MW01697872

Spectrum Test Prep

Grade 5

Test Preparation for:

Reading
Language
Math

Program Authors:
Dale Foreman
Alan C. Cohen
Jerome D. Kaplan
Ruth Mitchell

SPECTRUM
Grand Rapids, Michigan

Frank Schaffer Publications®

Send all inquiries to:
Frank Schaffer Publications
3195 Wilson Drive NW
Grand Rapids, Michigan 49534

Spectrum Test Prep—grade 5

ISBN 0-7696-3055-3

6 7 8 9 10 11 WAL 11 10 09 08 07 06

Table of Contents

Test Prep

The Program That Teaches Test-Taking Achievement

Spectrum is a well-known name in the test prep market. Over the years, we have identified the skills and strategies that students need to master the challenges of taking a standardized test. Becoming familiar with the test-taking experience can help ensure your child's success.

Test Prep covers all test skill areas

Test Prep contains the subject areas that are represented in the five major standardized tests. *Test Prep* will help your child prepare for the following tests:

- California Achievement Tests® (CAT/5)
- Comprehensive Tests of Basic Skills (CTBS/4)
- Iowa Tests of Basic Skills® (ITBS, Form K)
- Metropolitan Achievement Test (MAT/7)
- Stanford Achievement Test(SAT/9)

Test Prep provides strategies for success

Many students need special support when preparing to take a standardized test. *Test Prep* gives your child the opportunity to practice and become familiar with:

- General test content
- The test format
- Listening and following standard directions
- Working in structured settings
- Maintaining a silent, sustained effort
- Using test-taking strategies

Test Prep is comprehensive

Test Prep provides a complete presentation of the types of skills covered in standardized tests in a variety of formats. These formats are similar to those your child will encounter when testing. The subject areas covered in this book include:

- Reading
- Language
- Math

Test Prep gives students the practice they need

Each student lesson provides several components that help develop test-taking skills:

- An **Example,** with directions and sample test items
- A **Tips** feature, that gives test-taking strategies
- A **Practice** section, to help students practice answering questions in each test format

Each book gives focused test practice that builds confidence:

- A **Test Yourself** lesson for each unit gives students the opportunity to apply what they have learned in the unit.
- A **Test Practice** section gives students the experience of a longer test-like situation.
- A **Progress Chart** allows students to note and record their own progress.

Test Prep is the first and most successful program ever developed to help students become familiar with the test-taking experience. *Test Prep* can help to build self-confidence, reduce test anxiety, and provide the opportunity for students to successfully show what they have learned.

A Message to Parents and Teachers:

- **Standardized tests: the yardstick for your child's future**

  Standardized testing is one of the cornerstones of American education. From its beginning in the early part of this century, standardized testing has gradually become the yardstick by which student performance is judged. For better or worse, your child's future will be determined in great part by how well he or she performs on the standardized test used by your school district.

- **Even good students can have trouble with testing**

  In general, standardized tests are well designed and carefully developed to assess students' abilities in a consistent and balanced manner. However, there are many factors that can hinder the performance of an individual student when testing. These might include test anxiety, unfamiliarity with the test's format, or failure to understand the directions.

  In addition, it is rare that students are taught all of the material that appears on a standardized test. This is because the curriculum of most schools does not directly match the content of the standardized test. There will certainly be overlap between what your child learns in school and how he or she is tested, but some materials will probably be unfamiliar.

- **Ready to Test will lend a helping hand**

  It is because of the shortcomings of the standardized testing process that *Test Prep* was developed. The lessons in the book were created after a careful analysis of the most popular achievement tests. The items, while different from those on the tests, reflect the types of material that your child will encounter when testing. Students who use *Test Prep* will also become familiar with the format of the most popular achievement tests. This learning experience will reduce anxiety and give your child the opportunity to do his or her best on the next standardized test.

We urge you to review with your child the Message to Students and the feature "How to Use This Book" on pages 8-9. The information on these pages will help your child to use this book and develop important test-taking skills. We are confident that following the recommendations in this book will help your child to earn a test score that accurately reflects his or her true ability.

A Message to Students:

Frequently in school you will be asked to take a standardized achievement test. This test will show how much you know compared to other students in your grade. Your score on a standardized achievement test will help your teachers plan your education. It will also give you and your parents an idea of what your learning strengths and weaknesses are.

This book will help you do your best on a standardized achievement test. It will show you what to expect on the test and will give you a chance to practice important reading and test-taking skills. Here are some suggestions you can follow to make the best use of *Test Prep.*

Plan for success

- You'll do your best if you begin studying and do one or two lessons in this book each week. If you only have a little bit of time before a test is given, you can do one or two lessons each day.
- Study a little bit at a time, no more than 30 minutes a day. If you can, choose the same time each day to study in a quiet place.
- Keep a record of your score on each lesson. The charts on pp. 155 - 157 of this book will help you do this.

On the day of the test . . .

- Get a good night's sleep the night before the test. Have a light breakfast and lunch to keep from feeling drowsy during the test.
- Use the tips you learned in *Test Prep.* The most important tips are to skip difficult items, take the best guess when you're unsure of the answer, and try all the items.
- Don't worry if you are a little nervous when you take an achievement test. This is a natural feeling and may even help you stay alert.

How to Use This Book

1 *Getting Started*

Read the directions carefully.

Do the Sample item(s).

Read the Tips.

Lesson 2 Vocabulary Skills

Examples **Directions:** Read each item. Choose the answer that means the same or about the same as the underlined word.

A Load a barge

A car
B boat
C plane
D cart

B What is this car's maximum speed?

Maximum means —

F average
G normal
H lowest
J highest

Tips If you are not sure which answer is correct, take your best guess.

Practice

1 Jewelry made of coral

A a diamond
B a light plastic
C a hard sea deposit
D a type of glass

2 Adapt to conditions

F adjust
G accept
H agree
J allow

3 A large portion

A package
B serving
C table
D chair

4 Vivid dream

F frightening
G graphic
H long
J short

5 It was a crisp fall day.

Crisp means —

A brisk
B warm
C muggy
D windy

6 The beautiful schooner moved quickly.

A schooner is —

F an airplane
G a balloon
H a racing car
J a sailing ship

7 Lisa received an urgent message.

Urgent means —

A sad
B pressing
C exciting
D confusing

2 *Practice*

Complete the Practice items.

Continue working until you reach a Stop sign.

C muggy
D windy

2 Adapt to conditions

F adjust
G accept
H agree
J allow

3 A large portion

A package
B serving
C table
D chair

4 Vivid dream

F frightening
G graphic
H long
J short

6 The beautiful schooner moved quickly.

A schooner is —

F an airplane
G a balloon
H a racing car
J a sailing ship

7 Lisa received an urgent message.

Urgent means —

A sad
B pressing
C exciting
D confusing

14 STOP

ANSWER ROWS A ⒶⒷⒸⒹ 1 ⒶⒷⒸⒹ 3 ⒶⒷⒸⒹ 5 ⒶⒷⒸⒹ 7 ⒶⒷⒸⒹ
B ⒻⒼⒽⒿ 2 ⒻⒼⒽⒿ 4 ⒻⒼⒽⒿ 6 ⒻⒼⒽⒿ

3 *Check It Out*

Check your answers by turning to the Answer Keys at the back of the book.

Keep track of how you're doing by marking the number right on the Progress Charts on pages 155-157.

Mark the lesson you completed on the Table of Contents for each section.

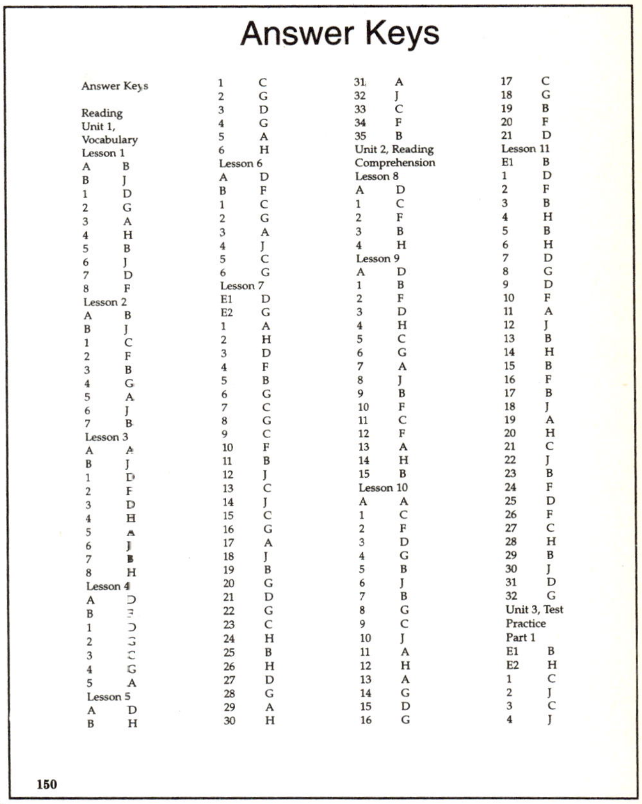

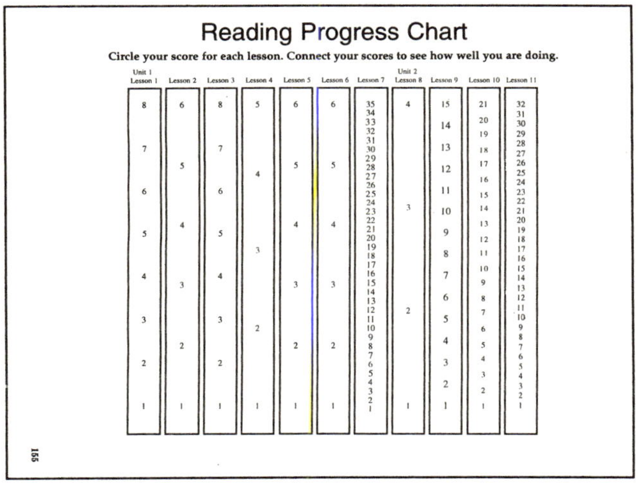

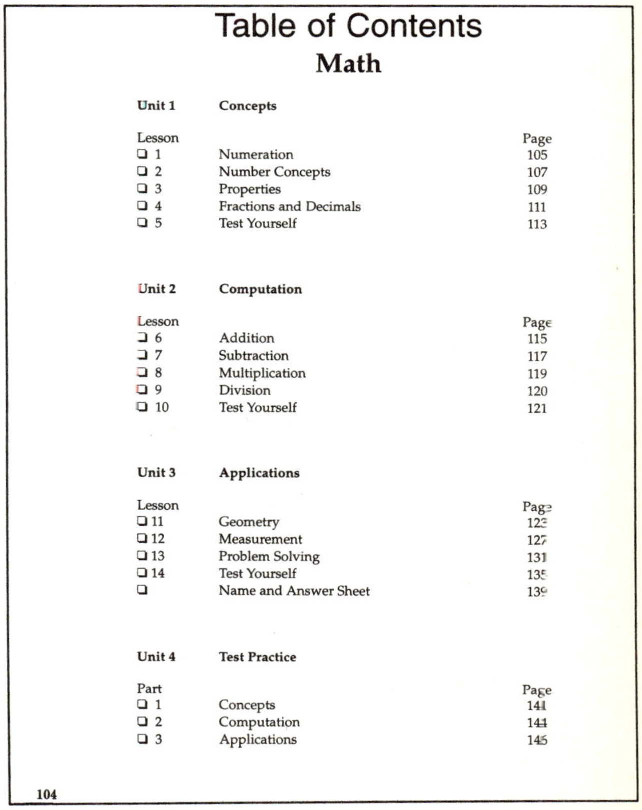

Skills

Reading

WORD ANALYSIS

Identifying initial consonant sounds
Matching vowel sounds
Identifying prefixes
Identifying root words
Identifying final consonant sounds
Identifying compound words
Identifying suffixes
Deriving affix meanings

VOCABULARY

Identifying synonyms
Identifying words with similar meanings
Identifying antonyms
Identifying multi-meaning words
Identifying words from a defining statement

READING COMPREHENSION

Recognizing story structures
Differentiating between fact and opinion
Making comparisons
Identifying story genres
Recognizing details
Understanding events
Drawing conclusions
Applying story information
Deriving word or phrase meaning
Understanding characters
Recognizing a narrator
Sequencing ideas
Making inferences
Labeling pictures
Generalizing from story information
Predicting from story content
Choosing the best title for a passage
Referring to a graphic
Understanding the author's purpose
Understanding feelings
Understanding the main idea

Language

LANGUAGE MECHANICS

Identifying the need for capital letters (proper nouns, beginning words) in sentences
Identifying the need for capital letters and punctuation marks in printed text
Identifying the need for punctuation marks (period, question mark, apostrophe, comma) in sentences

LANGUAGE EXPRESSION

Identifying the correct forms of nouns and pronouns
Identifying the correct forms of adjectives
Identifying correctly formed sentences
Sequencing sentences within a paragraph
Identifying the subject of a sentence
Combining sentences
Identifying the correct sentence to complete a paragraph
Identifying the predicate of a sentence
Identifying the correct forms of verbs
Identifying sentences that do not fit in a paragraph

SPELLING

Identifying correctly spelled words
Identifying incorrectly spelled words

Math

CONCEPTS

Recognizing ordinal position
Comparing and ordering whole numbers
Comparing sets
Sequencing numbers
Renaming numerals
Understanding place value
Recognizing fractional parts
Comparing and ordering fractions
Using operational symbols, words, and properties
Rounding
Using expanded notation
Using a number line
Grouping by 10s
Recognizing numerals
Skip counting by 10s
Recognizing visual and numeric patterns
Identifying fractions
Recognizing odd and even numbers
Regrouping
Estimating

COMPUTATION

Adding whole numbers, decimals, and fractions
Dividing whole numbers
Multiplying whole numbers
Subtracting whole numbers, decimals

APPLICATIONS

Finding perimeter and area
Solving oral and written word problems
Reading a calendar
Reading a thermometer
Recognizing plane and solid figures and their characteristics
Recognizing value of coins, bills, and money notation
Telling time
Identifying information needed to solve a problem
Estimating weight, size, and temperature
Understanding elapsed time
Understanding congruence, symmetry, and line segments
Understanding bar graphs, pictographs, and tables

Strategies

Following group directions
Utilizing test formats
Locating question and answer choices
Subvocalizing answer choices
Working methodically
Skipping difficult items and returning to them later
Identifying and using key words to find the answer
Staying with the first answer
Analyzing answer choices
Trying out answer choices
Eliminating answer choices
Restating a question
Substituting answer choices
Using logic
Using sentence context to find an answer
Referring to a passage to find the correct answer
Indicating that an item has no mistakes
Evaluating answer choices
Recalling the elements of a correctly formed sentence
Converting problems to a workable format
Noting the lettering of answer choices
Taking the best guess when unsure of the answer
Identifying and using key words, figures, and numbers
Marking the correct answer as soon as it is found
Adjusting to a structured setting
Maintaining a silent, sustained effort
Managing time effectively
Considering every answer choice
Computing carefully
Identifying the best test-taking strategy
Using context to find the answer
Locating the correct answer
Understanding unusual item formats
Following complex directions
Inferring word meaning from sentence context
Reasoning from facts and evidence
Encapsulating a passage
Skimming a passage
Avoiding over-analysis of answer choices
Recalling the function of verbs
Noting the differences among answer choices
Referring to a reference source
Recalling the elements of a correctly formed paragraph
Checking answers by the opposite operation
Finding the answer without computing
Performing the correct operation
Understanding oral questions
Indicating that the correct answer is not given

Table of Contents
Reading

Lesson 1 Synonyms

Examples

Directions: Read each item. Choose the word that means the same or about the same as the underlined word.

A resent a remark	**B Rapid means —**
A make	**F** foamy
B dislike	**G** weird
C appreciate	**H** short
D accept	**J** quick

Tips Be careful. The letters for the answer choices change for each question. Make sure the space you fill in matches the answer you think is correct.

Practice

1 expect a package

A ship
B lose
C replace
D anticipate

2 fond recollection

F attitude
G memory
H friend
J accomplishment

3 barren area

A empty
B hot
C large
D distant

4 delightful trip

F boring
G annoying
H pleasant
J expensive

5 To intend is to —

A resist
B plan
C pay
D dislike

6 An awkward person is —

F smart
G cranky
H skilled
J clumsy

7 To revolve is to —

A jump
B fly
C fall
D turn

8 To graze is to —

F eat
G run
H stand
J sit

STOP

ANSWER ROWS

A Ⓐ Ⓑ Ⓒ Ⓓ	1 Ⓐ Ⓑ Ⓒ Ⓓ	3 Ⓐ Ⓑ Ⓒ Ⓓ	5 Ⓐ Ⓑ Ⓒ Ⓓ	7 Ⓐ Ⓑ Ⓒ Ⓓ
B Ⓕ Ⓖ Ⓗ Ⓙ	2 Ⓕ Ⓖ Ⓗ Ⓙ	4 Ⓕ Ⓖ Ⓗ Ⓙ	6 Ⓕ Ⓖ Ⓗ Ⓙ	8 Ⓕ Ⓖ Ⓗ Ⓙ

Lesson 2 Vocabulary Skills

Examples

Directions: Read each item. Choose the answer that means the same or about the same as the underlined word.

A **Load a barge**

- **A** car
- **B** boat
- **C** plane
- **D** cart

B **What is this car's maximum speed?**

Maximum means —

- **F** average
- **G** normal
- **H** lowest
- **J** highest

Tips **If you are not sure which answer is correct, take your best guess.**

Practice

1 **Jewelry made of coral**

- **A** a diamond
- **B** a light plastic
- **C** a hard sea deposit
- **D** a type of glass

2 **Adapt to conditions**

- **F** adjust
- **G** accept
- **H** agree
- **J** allow

3 **A large portion**

- **A** package
- **B** serving
- **C** table
- **D** chair

4 **Vivid dream**

- **F** frightening
- **G** graphic
- **H** long
- **J** short

5 **It was a crisp fall day.**

Crisp means —

- **A** brisk
- **B** warm
- **C** muggy
- **D** windy

6 **The beautiful schooner moved quickly.**

A schooner is —

- **F** an airplane
- **G** a balloon
- **H** a racing car
- **J** a sailing ship

7 **Lisa received an urgent message.**

Urgent means —

- **A** sad
- **B** pressing
- **C** exciting
- **D** confusing

STOP

ANSWER ROWS A Ⓐ Ⓑ Ⓒ Ⓓ 1 Ⓐ Ⓑ Ⓒ Ⓓ 3 Ⓐ Ⓑ Ⓒ Ⓓ 5 Ⓐ Ⓑ Ⓒ Ⓓ 7 Ⓐ Ⓑ Ⓒ Ⓓ
B Ⓕ Ⓖ Ⓗ Ⓙ 2 Ⓕ Ⓖ Ⓗ Ⓙ 4 Ⓕ Ⓖ Ⓗ Ⓙ 6 Ⓕ Ⓖ Ⓗ Ⓙ

Examples

Directions: Read each item. Choose the answer that means the opposite of the underlined word.

A **limp flowers**

- **A** stiff
- **B** uncut
- **C** beautiful
- **D** sagging

B **an obvious solution**

- **F** recent
- **G** clear
- **H** new
- **J** hidden

Tips

If a question is too difficult, skip it and come back to it later, if you have time.

Practice

1 **the enormous bug**

- **A** dangerous
- **B** harmless
- **C** huge
- **D** tiny

2 **liberate people**

- **F** imprison
- **G** scare
- **H** warn
- **J** free

3 **considerate friend**

- **A** attentive
- **B** new
- **C** impatient
- **D** thoughtless

4 **the initial idea**

- **F** worst
- **G** best
- **H** last
- **J** first

5 **casual party**

- **A** formal
- **B** easy
- **C** comfortable
- **D** exciting

6 **sensible idea**

- **F** intelligent
- **G** wonderful
- **H** common
- **J** foolish

7 **cruel comments**

- **A** harsh
- **B** kind
- **C** amazing
- **D** cautious

8 **skillful performance**

- **F** fine
- **G** talented
- **H** clumsy
- **J** angry

STOP

ANSWER ROWS
A Ⓐ Ⓑ Ⓒ Ⓓ 1 Ⓐ Ⓑ Ⓒ Ⓓ 3 Ⓐ Ⓑ Ⓒ Ⓓ 5 Ⓐ Ⓑ Ⓒ Ⓓ 7 Ⓐ Ⓑ Ⓒ Ⓓ
B Ⓕ Ⓖ Ⓗ Ⓙ 2 Ⓕ Ⓖ Ⓗ Ⓙ 4 Ⓕ Ⓖ Ⓗ Ⓙ 6 Ⓕ Ⓖ Ⓗ Ⓙ 8 Ⓕ Ⓖ Ⓗ Ⓙ

Examples

Directions: Read each item. Choose the answer you think is correct.

A **The baby has dark brown curls.**

In which sentence does the word curls mean the same thing as in the sentence above?

A English ivy curls around the window.
B The power cord lay in curls everywhere.
C The newspaper curls up in wet weather.
D After her haircut, curls covered the floor.

B **Where should I _______ this letter?**

Use a _______ to smooth the edge.

F file
G place
H plane
J keep

Tips

Read the question carefully. Use the meaning of the sentences to find the right answer.

Practice

1 **Irene decided to wash the car.**

In which sentence does the word wash mean the same thing as in the sentence above?

A We separated the wash into three piles.
B The river might wash out the dam.
C The storm flooded the dry wash.
D No one wanted to wash the dishes.

2 **The last step is to check for errors.**

In which sentence does the word step mean the same thing as in the sentence above?

F Please step over here, next to the door.
G She followed every step in the directions.
H The top step was covered with ice.
J "Step this way!" the guide told us.

3 **My cousins live on this _______ .**

Don't _______ the aisle near the door.

A street
B sit in
C block
D walk in

4 **The _______ has a strong arm.**

That _______ is for orange juice.

F player
G pitcher
H bottle
J team

5 **What _______ does Carl work?**

Help me _______ the box to that side.

A shift
B time
C move
D job

STOP

ANSWER ROWS A Ⓐ Ⓑ Ⓒ Ⓓ 1 Ⓐ Ⓑ Ⓒ Ⓓ 3 Ⓐ Ⓑ Ⓒ Ⓓ 5 Ⓐ Ⓑ Ⓒ Ⓓ
B Ⓕ Ⓖ Ⓗ Ⓙ 2 Ⓕ Ⓖ Ⓗ Ⓙ 4 Ⓕ Ⓖ Ⓗ Ⓙ

Examples

Directions: Read the paragraph. Find the word below the paragraph that fits best in each numbered blank.

Walking is one of the most ___(A)___ activities you can do. A brisk walk strengthens your legs, heart, and circulatory system. It's also a good way to relax and ___(B)___ your attitude.

A
- **A** exercising
- **B** fearsome
- **C** sincere
- **D** beneficial

B
- **F** rest
- **G** assert
- **H** improve
- **J** insist

Tips

Look for the answer that makes the most sense with the other words in the passage.

Practice

Keeping a house warm in winter and cool in summer is a ___(1)___ expense for a family. There are a few ___(2)___ things you can do, however, that will save a great deal of money. Keep your doors closed except when they are being used. ___(3)___ small openings around windows and doors with caulk. Use at least twelve inches of insulation in your ___(4)___ or crawlspace. These three suggestions can ___(5)___ your ___(6)___ energy bill by as much as twenty percent.

1
- **A** small
- **B** cost
- **C** major
- **D** reasonable

2
- **F** more
- **G** simple
- **H** difficult
- **J** insistent

3
- **A** Build
- **B** Crack
- **C** Find
- **D** Seal

4
- **F** room
- **G** attic
- **H** outside
- **J** hall

5
- **A** reduce
- **B** increase
- **C** average
- **D** relax

6
- **F** rare
- **G** occasional
- **H** typical
- **J** frequent

STOP

ANSWER ROWS
A Ⓐ Ⓑ Ⓒ Ⓓ 1 Ⓐ Ⓑ Ⓒ Ⓓ 3 Ⓐ Ⓑ Ⓒ Ⓓ 5 Ⓐ Ⓑ Ⓒ Ⓓ
B Ⓕ Ⓖ Ⓗ Ⓙ 2 Ⓕ Ⓖ Ⓗ Ⓙ 4 Ⓕ Ⓖ Ⓗ Ⓙ 6 Ⓕ Ⓖ Ⓗ Ⓙ

Examples

Directions: Read each question. Fill in the circle for the answer you think is correct.

A Which of these words probably comes from the Latin word *finire* meaning *to end*?

A finer
B finger
C fire
D finish

B Once we were safely inside, I heard Jorge ________ the door.

Which of these words would indicate that Jorge locked the door?

F bolt
G close
H slam
J fix

Tips

Read each question carefully. Be sure you understand what you are supposed to do before choosing your answer.

Practice

1 Which of these words probably comes from the Latin word *collum* meaning *neck*?

A collect
B college
C collar
D calm

2 Which of these words probably comes from the Old English word *cwacian* meaning *to shake*?

F quick
G quake
H creek
J chew

3 The field trip was ________ to thirty students.

Which of these words means the number of students was restricted?

A limited
B cancelled
C sampled
D remarked

4 The butterfly ________ from the cocoon.

Which of these words would indicate that the butterfly came out of the cocoon?

F reflected
G shaped
H furnished
J emerged

For numbers 5 and 6, choose the answer that best defines the underlined part.

5 artist realist

A type of
B able to
C person who
D always

6 intercept international

F opposite of
G between
H recently
J government

STOP

ANSWER ROWS
A Ⓐ Ⓑ Ⓒ Ⓓ 1 Ⓐ Ⓑ Ⓒ Ⓓ 3 Ⓐ Ⓑ Ⓒ Ⓓ 5 Ⓐ Ⓑ Ⓒ Ⓓ
B Ⓕ Ⓖ Ⓗ Ⓙ 2 Ⓕ Ⓖ Ⓗ Ⓙ 4 Ⓕ Ⓖ Ⓗ Ⓙ 6 Ⓕ Ⓖ Ⓗ Ⓙ

Examples

Directions: Find the word or words that mean the same or almost the same as the underlined word.

E1 alter a suit

A purchase
B damage
C inspect
D change

E2 Which of these probably comes from the Old English word *græppian* meaning *to seize*?

F grape
G grasp
H eager
J grim

For numbers 1-8, find the word or words that mean the same or almost the same as the underlined word.

1 assemble a machine

A put together
B take apart
C operate
D repair

2 lasting solution

F temporary
G difficult
H permanent
J apparent

3 open a cabinet

A large box
B kitchen drawer
C wooden door
D storage cupboard

4 an exciting period

F length of time
G short story
H vacation
J game

5 An avenue is the same as a—

A manor
B street
C park
D sign

6 Something that is essential is —

F extra
G important
H special
J warm

7 A puzzle is like a —

A sport
B project
C problem
D battle

8 If something is flimsy it is —

F bitter
G weak
H strong
J tired

GO

ANSWER ROWS
E1 Ⓐ Ⓑ Ⓒ Ⓓ 1 Ⓐ Ⓑ Ⓒ Ⓓ 3 Ⓐ Ⓑ Ⓒ Ⓓ 5 Ⓐ Ⓑ Ⓒ Ⓓ 7 Ⓐ Ⓑ Ⓒ Ⓓ
E2 Ⓕ Ⓖ Ⓗ Ⓙ 2 Ⓕ Ⓖ Ⓗ Ⓙ 4 Ⓕ Ⓖ Ⓗ Ⓙ 6 Ⓕ Ⓖ Ⓗ Ⓙ 8 Ⓕ Ⓖ Ⓗ Ⓙ

9 **The weary traveler reached her home.**

Weary means —

A refreshed
B excited
C tired
D worried

10 **She was thrilled to have a chance to conduct the orchestra.**

Conduct means —

F lead
G join
H tell
J name

11 **The day turned out to be pleasant.**

Pleasant means —

A unhappy
B enjoyable
C exciting
D surprising

12 **When the door opened it startled me.**

Startled means —

F angered
G tired
H pleased
J surprised

13 **The teacher was pleased with my accurate answer.**

Accurate means —

A honest
B long
C correct
D careless

For numbers 14-19, find the word that means the opposite of the underlined word.

14 **being humble**

F quiet
G angry
H sensitive
J proud

15 **outskirts of town**

A edge
B suburbs
C center
D regions

16 **hostile people**

F pleasant
G friendly
H warlike
J quiet

17 **irritate her eyes**

A soothe
B cover
C shade
D close

18 **wonderful triumph**

F victory
G experience
H contest
J loss

19 **successful business**

A profitable
B failing
C national
D local

GO

ANSWER ROWS
9 Ⓐ Ⓑ Ⓒ Ⓓ 11 Ⓐ Ⓑ Ⓒ Ⓓ 13 Ⓐ Ⓑ Ⓒ Ⓓ 15 Ⓐ Ⓑ Ⓒ Ⓓ 17 Ⓐ Ⓑ Ⓒ Ⓓ 19 Ⓐ Ⓑ Ⓒ Ⓓ
10 Ⓕ Ⓖ Ⓗ Ⓙ 12 Ⓕ Ⓖ Ⓗ Ⓙ 14 Ⓕ Ⓖ Ⓗ Ⓙ 16 Ⓕ Ⓖ Ⓗ Ⓙ 18 Ⓕ Ⓖ Ⓗ Ⓙ

For numbers 20–23, choose the word that correctly completes both sentences.

20 Whose ________ is it?

Be sure to ________ the water off.

- **F** shut
- **G** turn
- **H** place
- **J** position

21 The ________ crossed the bridge.

You will have to ________ hard for the race.

- **A** bus
- **B** prepare
- **C** compete
- **D** train

22 Who will keep you ________ on the trip?

Her ________ makes computers.

- **F** entertained
- **G** company
- **H** business
- **J** factory

23 We heard a great ________ last night.

A metal ________ went around the tree.

- **A** record
- **B** strap
- **C** band
- **D** concert

24 | **I used a rubber patch to fix my bike tire.** |

In which sentence does the word patch mean the same thing as in the sentence above?

- **F** The rabbit ran into that big briar patch.
- **G** Can they patch things up after the fight?
- **H** Reg sewed a patch over the hole in his pants.
- **J** A patch of blue appeared in the clouds.

25 | **My sketch was better than I thought.** |

In which sentence does the word sketch mean the same thing as in the sentence above?

- **A** My favorite comedians did a funny sketch on TV last night.
- **B** She wanted a sketch of her new house.
- **C** The boy who saw the accident had to sketch in details for the police.
- **D** We will sketch our pets in art class.

For numbers 26 and 27, choose the answer that best defines the underlined part.

26 Russian Hungarian

- **F** place near
- **G** near
- **H** person from
- **J** well-known

27 readjust recapture

- **A** like
- **B** same as
- **C** difficult
- **D** again

GO

ANSWER ROWS 20 Ⓕ Ⓖ Ⓗ Ⓙ 22 Ⓕ Ⓖ Ⓗ Ⓙ 24 Ⓕ Ⓖ Ⓗ Ⓙ 26 Ⓕ Ⓖ Ⓗ Ⓙ
21 Ⓐ Ⓑ Ⓒ Ⓓ 23 Ⓐ Ⓑ Ⓒ Ⓓ 25 Ⓐ Ⓑ Ⓒ Ⓓ 27 Ⓐ Ⓑ Ⓒ Ⓓ

28 Which of these words probably comes from the Middle English word *facioun* meaning *manner*?

- **F** flash
- **G** fashion
- **H** face
- **J** faith

29 Which of these words probably comes from the German word *schichten* meaning *to arrange in order*?

- **A** shift
- **B** chief
- **C** charge
- **D** shelf

30 The pilot ________ the announcement about when we were going to land.

Which of these words means the pilot made the announcement again?

- **F** landed
- **G** argued
- **H** repeated
- **J** raised

31 The ingredients were ________ together.

Which of these words means the ingredients were mixed together?

- **A** blended
- **B** baked
- **C** stored
- **D** purchased

Read the paragraph. Find the word below the paragraph that fits best in each numbered blank.

Home improvement "superstores" are now __(32)__ in large cities throughout America. These stores __(33)__ everything for the person who wants to fix up a house or apartment, from nails to entire kitchens. To shop in one of these stores, you need at least a shopping cart, and sometimes a heavy-duty hand truck. The __(34)__ in the superstores are specially trained to help customers find what they are looking for in these __(35)__ hardware stores.

32
- **F** avoided
- **G** replaced
- **H** exceeded
- **J** found

33
- **A** restrain
- **B** prevent
- **C** carry
- **D** acquire

34
- **F** personnel
- **G** shelves
- **H** customers
- **J** alternatives

35
- **A** inferior
- **B** mammoth
- **C** uneventful
- **D** mere

STOP

ANSWER ROWS 28 Ⓕ Ⓖ Ⓗ Ⓙ 30 Ⓕ Ⓖ Ⓗ Ⓙ 32 Ⓕ Ⓖ Ⓗ Ⓙ 34 Ⓕ Ⓖ Ⓗ Ⓙ
29 Ⓐ Ⓑ Ⓒ Ⓓ 31 Ⓐ Ⓑ Ⓒ Ⓓ 33 Ⓐ Ⓑ Ⓒ Ⓓ 35 Ⓐ Ⓑ Ⓒ Ⓓ

NUMBER RIGHT ______

Lesson 8 Critical Reading

Example

Directions: Read each item. Choose the answer you think is correct. Mark the space for your answer.

The desert stretched for countless miles before the travelers. It was dotted with huge dunes formed by the wind that seemed to blow forever. The six families knew the next few days were going to be the most difficult yet.

A What part of a story does this passage tell about?

A the plot
B the characters
C the mood
D the setting

Tips Look for key words in the question. These key words will help you understand the question and find the right answer.

Practice

1 Which of these probably came from a newspaper article?

A Avondo stood on the mountain peak and commanded the storm to stop.

B It was a huge rain storm that brought the family together.

C Traffic was stopped on the expressway because of flooding from the storm.

D Storms often follow the jet stream from west to east across the United States.

2 Which of these statements from a biography expresses an opinion?

F Ms. Lyle practices harder than most other performers.

G Her career began with a performance at Carnegie Hall.

H The audience was the largest in the history of the hall.

J Louisa's grandparents arrived in America with less than ten dollars.

3 The earthquake had thrown an unlikely group of people together, from a homeless man starting his first day on a new job to a doctor on her way to a national conference.

What part of a story does this passage tell about?

A the plot

B the characters

C the mood

D the setting

4 Which of these statements from a magazine article expresses a fact?

F Both candidates responded poorly to the questions from the audience.

G It is unlikely that higher taxes will benefit the people who pay them.

H Fewer than 40 percent of the people in the county voted last week.

J Voters usually support the candidate who looks best on television.

STOP

ANSWER ROWS A Ⓐ Ⓑ Ⓒ Ⓓ 2 Ⓕ Ⓖ Ⓗ Ⓙ 4 Ⓕ Ⓖ Ⓗ Ⓙ
1 Ⓐ Ⓑ Ⓒ Ⓓ 3 Ⓐ Ⓑ Ⓒ Ⓓ

Example

Directions: Read the passage. Find the best answer to the questions that follow the passage.

Lona arrived at the theatre early, hoping she could get a good seat. She was surprised to see that lots of other people had the same idea. The line was four blocks long! She sighed and took her place at the end of the line. Then, after a twenty minute wait, the manager came out of the theatre and announced that the show was sold out.	**A Lona discovered that the —** **A** manager was angry. **B** movie probably wasn't very good. **C** whole school had the same idea. **D** ticket line was awfully long.

Tips Look for key words in the question, then find the same words in the passage. This will help you locate the correct answer.

Practice

Here is a passage about a birthday surprise that most young people would enjoy. Read the passage and then do numbers 1 through 7 on page 25.

"Can't you tell me yet what the surprise is?"

"No, we can't. Just relax and enjoy the scenery. We'll be there soon enough. With all your talking, I can't concentrate on my driving."

"Your mother is right. It won't be a surprise if we tell you. Trust me; you'll think it is wonderful."

Edward looked at his sister Lee Ann and shrugged his shoulders. They weren't going to tell him about the surprise. Even whining didn't work. He was so excited he felt he could explode, but there was nothing he could do about it.

In about fifteen minutes, the car pulled into a large field. Some people in the field were unloading a huge basket from a truck. Edward wondered if this was part of the surprise.

The family got out of the car and walked over to the people by the basket. Edward still didn't know what was going on. Then he saw the huge, colorful cloth on the ground. His birthday surprise was a ride in a hot air balloon!

Edward watched the crew turn the basket on its side and attach it to the balloon. They then turned on a powerful burner that forced hot air into the balloon. The hot air slowly filled the balloon and it began to rise above the basket. After about fifteen minutes, the balloon was floating above them and it had brought the basket right-side up.

"Okay, folks. We're ready. Just climb in and we'll take off."

Edward went in first. After all, it was his birthday. His father helped his mother and sister into the basket and then climbed in himself. The pilot shouted "Weight Off" and threw some sandbags to the ground. The crew let go of the lines and the balloon floated into the sky.

GO

1 How did Edward feel during the car ride?

A Angry

B Excited

C Eager

D Puzzled

2 During the balloon ride, the family will be in a —

F basket.

G cloth bag.

H wooden box.

J small room.

3 Which of these is not explained in the passage?

A How the balloon arrived

B How the family arrived

C How the balloon is filled

D How the balloon is steered

4 Who is driving the car?

F Edward

G Lee Ann

H Mother

J Father

5 What does the expression "Weight Off" mean?

A One person should climb out of the balloon.

B The balloon has filled and the basket has turned right-side up.

C The pilot is ready to take off.

D It's time to light the burner.

6 When the family arrived—

F the balloon was already filled with hot air and was floating above the basket.

G some people were unloading a basket from a truck.

H the pilot was throwing sandbags from the basket to the ground.

J the balloon crew was preparing a surprise party.

7 In the last paragraph, the word *lines* refers to —

A ropes that keep the balloon from floating away.

B a large number of people waiting to ride in the balloon.

C marks on paper that show you where to write something.

D marks on the ground where the balloon is supposed to land.

GO

ANSWER ROWS A Ⓐ Ⓑ Ⓒ Ⓓ 2 Ⓕ Ⓖ Ⓗ Ⓙ 4 Ⓕ Ⓖ Ⓗ Ⓙ 6 Ⓕ Ⓖ Ⓗ Ⓙ

1 Ⓐ Ⓑ Ⓒ Ⓓ 3 Ⓐ Ⓑ Ⓒ Ⓓ 5 Ⓐ Ⓑ Ⓒ Ⓓ 7 Ⓐ Ⓑ Ⓒ Ⓓ

Cats Great and Small

The cat that purrs sweetly when you scratch its chin is a close cousin of the lions that roam the plains of Africa and other great cats. All cats belong to the Felidae family, whose members can be found in every region of the globe except Antarctica. They are skilled hunters, and even the tamest cat will fall into a crouch if a mouse or other small animal is nearby.

Scientists believe that small, wild cats were captured and kept as pets by people as long as 10,000 years ago. The Egyptians were the first to breed cats and, for a time, cats were thought by Egyptians to be holy. As civilization spread from the Middle East to other parts of the world, cats followed. Today, cats are the most popular pet in both America and Western Europe. They are less popular in other parts of the world, and are often thought of as being pests.

The body temperature of a cat is about 101°, which is a few degrees warmer than humans. Cats are very sensitive to the temperature around them, and as the temperature rises above 95°, they pant to keep cool.

Cats have keen eyesight and have developed the ability to see well in the dark. They also have a good sense of hearing and can hear sounds beyond the range of humans. Unlike dogs, a cat's sense of smell is not particularly good.

Anyone who is familiar with both cats and dogs knows that dogs are more easily trained and seem to be more loyal. These differences can be traced to the origins of both animals. The wild ancestors of dogs were pack animals in which loyalty to the group and cooperative behavior were important for survival. The ancestors of cats were more solitary and independent, so the domestic cats of today seem less affectionate than dogs.

Another important difference between cats and dogs is that there are fewer breeds of cats. In addition, the differences among breeds are smaller than among breeds of dogs. For example, a small breed of dog may be one tenth the size of a large breed and may have much different features. Cats are all about the same size and their ears, coats, tails, and other features are very similar.

GO

8 Where would a passage like this be most likely to appear?

F In an almanac

G In a dictionary

H In a book about history

J In an encyclopedia

9 What does it mean to say that a cat will "fall into a crouch"?

A It is tired.

B It is ready to hunt.

C It is ready to purr.

D It is afraid.

10 How did cats get from the Middle East to Europe?

F They followed people as they moved or they were brought by people.

G They were there before the people moved from the Middle East.

H The Egyptians bred them.

J Cats originated in Europe.

11 What happens to cats if the temperature gets too high?

A They sweat just like people.

B Their body temperature falls.

C They begin breathing heavily.

D They become sensitive to the temperature.

12 Which part of the passage describes why cats seem less loyal than dogs?

F The ancestors of cats were more solitary and independent...

G The Egyptians were the first to breed cats...

H Unlike dogs, a cat's sense of smell is not particularly good.

J Cats are very sensitive to the temperature around them.

13 In the fifth paragraph, what does the phrase "pack animals" mean?

A Animals that stay in groups

B Good hunters

C Animals that carry things

D Animals that hunt by themselves

14 When compared with dogs, cats have —

F poor vision.

G good vision.

H a poor sense of smell.

J a keen sense of smell.

15 Who belongs to the Felidae family?

A Only domestic cats

B All cats

C Only wild cats

D All cats and dogs

STOP

ANSWER ROWS 8 Ⓕ Ⓖ Ⓗ Ⓙ 10 Ⓕ Ⓖ Ⓗ Ⓙ 12 Ⓕ Ⓖ Ⓗ Ⓙ 14 Ⓕ Ⓖ Ⓗ Ⓙ
9 Ⓐ Ⓑ Ⓒ Ⓓ 11 Ⓐ Ⓑ Ⓒ Ⓓ 13 Ⓐ Ⓑ Ⓒ Ⓓ 15 Ⓐ Ⓑ Ⓒ Ⓓ

Example

Directions: Read each passage. Find the best answer to the questions that follow the passage.

Joe started down the ladder. He had just finished painting the window frame and he wanted to see if he had missed any spots. As he was about to step off the ladder, his knee bumped it slightly. It was just enough to send the can of paint spinning through the air. In seconds, paint was everywhere, on the ceiling, the walls, and the floor.

A As the can fell, Joe probably felt —

A powerless.

B proud of his work.

C pleased.

D like he had won something.

Tips

Skim the passage then read the questions. Refer back to the passage to find the answers to the questions.

Practice

Here is a passage about someone whose characters are very famous. Read the passage and then do numbers 1 through 7 on page 29.

Almost no young people today know who the cartoon character Oswald the Rabbit was, but they certainly recognize his successor, Bugs Bunny. Oswald, Bugs, and hundreds of other characters were created by Walt Disney, perhaps the most famous cartoonist in history.

Born in Chicago in 1901, Walt Disney always wanted to be an artist. After returning from World War I, in which he drove an ambulance, Disney worked as a commercial artist. He enjoyed drawing cartoons more than anything else, and decided to try his hand at a technology that was new at the time, moving pictures.

In the 1920's, he produced several films where he made cartoon characters move as if by magic. The technique Disney used was painstaking. He made hundreds or even thousands of repeated drawings of the same character. In each drawing, the character was changed just a bit. A film was taken of the series of drawings, and when it was shown, the characters appeared to move. The process, called animation, is still used today, although computers have made the process much easier.

In 1928, Disney created his most famous character, Mortimer Mouse, who we know today as Mickey. The mouse starred in a cartoon called *Steamboat Willie*, which was unusual because it involved the use of a sound track. Within the next few years, Disney invented many of his other characters.

The list of Disney's animation successes is long and memorable. It includes *Pinocchio*, *Dumbo*, *Bambi*, *Cinderella*, and *Peter Pan*. Perhaps his most remarkable animated film was *Snow White and the Seven Dwarfs*. Created in 1937, it was an immediate success. Today, more than fifty years later, it is still one of the most popular films for children.

GO

1 What is one of the chief differences between animation today and in Walt Disney's early years?

- **A** More people like animated movies.
- **B** Fewer people like animated movies.
- **C** Computers have made the job easier.
- **D** Computers have made the job harder.

2 Which of these words best describes Walt Disney?

- **F** Creative
- **G** Athletic
- **H** Exciting
- **J** Quiet

3 What makes the film *Snow White* so remarkable?

- **A** It was a great success.
- **B** It took more than a year to make.
- **C** It was made at a time when there were no computers.
- **D** It has remained popular for more than fifty years.

4 The author of this passage would probably agree that —

- **F** Oswald Rabbit is well-known today.
- **G** Walt Disney was a remarkable person.
- **H** animation is an easy technique.
- **J** cartoons move by magic.

5 In the third paragraph, what is the meaning of the word "painstaking"?

- **A** Something that hurts because it involves hard work
- **B** Something that takes a long time and involves much hard work
- **C** Requiring a lot of effort, like running a marathon
- **D** Requiring many fine tools, such as pens and pencils

6 The secret of animation is to —

- **F** make drawings that are exactly alike, then film them.
- **G** choose names for characters that make people remember them.
- **H** combine music, voices, and sound effects with pictures.
- **J** make a film of many drawings that change just a little.

7 Which of these descriptions of the passage best supports your answer for number 6?

- **A** The passage describes how Walt Disney became a cartoonist.
- **B** The passage explains in detail how animation is done.
- **C** The passage describes some of Walt Disney's most famous characters.
- **D** The passage talks about the use of computers for animation.

GO

ANSWER ROWS
A Ⓐ Ⓑ Ⓒ Ⓓ 2 Ⓕ Ⓖ Ⓗ Ⓙ 4 Ⓕ Ⓖ Ⓗ Ⓙ 6 Ⓕ Ⓖ Ⓗ Ⓙ
1 Ⓐ Ⓑ Ⓒ Ⓓ 3 Ⓐ Ⓑ Ⓒ Ⓓ 5 Ⓐ Ⓑ Ⓒ Ⓓ 7 Ⓐ Ⓑ Ⓒ Ⓓ

How did we get our alphabet?

The first writing that humans did was picture drawing. Primitive humans drew pictures of animals, hunts, storms, and other things that were important to them. These pictures have been found all around the world.

The Egyptians were probably the first people who recorded events in an organized manner. More than 5,000 years ago they started using hieroglyphics, which means "sacred writings." A hieroglyphic is a picture or symbol of a person, thing, or event. As new words were invented, more pictures were needed. The Egyptians' language grew larger and larger, so finding pictures for all the words became difficult.

The Phoenicians had a different idea. About 3,000 years ago, the Phoenicians were great sailors and traders. They traveled to many places and needed a way to keep track of their business transactions. They were the first to use symbols to represent sounds. The first letter of the Phoenician alphabet was called *aleph*. The second letter was *beth*. They were similar to our letters A and B, so in a sense, the Phoenicians even gave us the word alphabet!

The Greeks adopted the Phoenician alphabet and changed it to fit their language. They added the vowels. Later, the Romans took the Greek alphabet and changed it again to suit their language, which was Latin. Our alphabet is close to the Latin alphabet. The letter J was the last addition to the alphabet we use now; it came in the fifteenth century. Our alphabet has not changed in 500 years.

Here is an interesting alphabet story. The Egyptian civilization that developed the first picture writings died out, but their hieroglyphics carved on rocks and written on papyrus remained. No one knew what the hieroglyphics meant until 1799, when a soldier found a stone that explained their "codes." It was found near the Egyptian village of Rosetta and was called the Rosetta Stone. The stone contained Egyptian picture writing and Greek words side by side, and it said that the two were the same. This helped people figure out what the Egyptian pictures meant exactly.

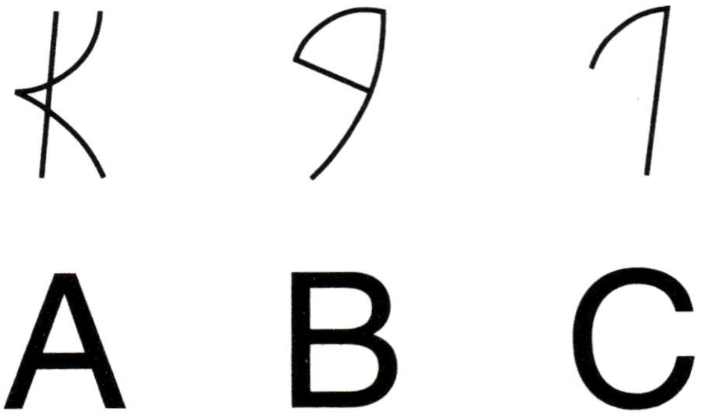

GO

8 According to the article, who invented a way to represent sounds?

F The Latins

G The Phoenicians

H The Greeks

J The Romans

9 At first, writing was mostly about —

A symbols for sounds.

B vowels and consonants.

C important things.

D ancient civilizations.

10 The Phoenicians needed writing because they were —

F warriors.

G well educated people.

H inventors of the Rosetta Stone.

J sailors and traders.

11 If you wanted to figure out a message in code, it would be helpful to have something like the —

A Rosetta Stone.

B Egyptian hieroglyphics.

C vowels added by the Greeks.

D modern alphabet.

12 A great advantage of an alphabet over picture writing is that —

F pictures must be drawn or written.

G an alphabet can begin and end with any letter you want.

H letters and words can be used to describe many things.

J an alphabet can be written, but a picture must be carved in stone.

13 The passage gives you enough evidence to believe that —

A people often adopt previous inventions and change them to suit their needs.

B if someone had not invented writing, there could be no business today.

C the Egyptians were the smartest people because they invented picture writing.

D no one could have invented writing until paper was invented first.

14 The boxes below show some events described in the article.

1	2	3
Egyptians used hieroglyphics	Phoenicians used symbols for sounds	

Which of these belongs in Box 3?

F The Phoenicians were traders.

G The Rosetta Stone was discovered.

H The Egyptians invented papyrus.

J The Egyptians invented Latin.

GO

ANSWER ROWS 8 Ⓕ Ⓖ Ⓗ Ⓙ 10 Ⓕ Ⓖ Ⓗ Ⓙ 12 Ⓕ Ⓖ Ⓗ Ⓙ 14 Ⓕ Ⓖ Ⓗ Ⓙ
9 Ⓐ Ⓑ Ⓒ Ⓓ 11 Ⓐ Ⓑ Ⓒ Ⓓ 13 Ⓐ Ⓑ Ⓒ Ⓓ

Helios and Phaethon

The people who lived in Greece long ago had good lives, but they didn't know many things that people know today. They wondered about the sun, the moon, the stars, the seasons, and all sorts of things. The Greeks made up stories to explain some of these things. Gods and goddesses were characters in these stories, and they could do magical deeds. Many people believed in the gods and goddesses then, but few people do today. Even so, the Greek stories, or myths, are still interesting to read and tell.

One Greek myth is about the sun god Helios. His job was to control the powerful horses that pulled the sun across the sky every day. They would start out in the east and pull the big, fiery ball across the heavens and drop down to earth in the west. The horses were so big and strong that the only one able to drive them was Helios.

Helios had a young son, Phaethon, who wanted to drive the sun chariot. "Please, Father, let me drive," he begged every day. "I've been helping around the stables. I can drive those horses around. I'm big enough."

One day Helios finally agreed. He went out and harnessed the horses to the sun chariot. "Drive carefully, Son," he said. Helios watched them leave.

The horses knew the way because they made the journey every day. On this day, something seemed different to them. Phaethon wasn't handling the reins the same as usual. The horses went too fast, and the boy pulled wildly on the reins and yelled. Then the horses went too low. They let the sun get so close to earth that it became burned in places. In other spots the sun chariot was so far away that the earth became icy cold.

The young Phaethon finally made it home. He was very glad to give the job of driving the horses back to his father. "I am sorry, Father. I wasn't strong enough to do your job."

The Greeks used the story of Phaethon to explain deserts and the polar regions. They believed that the places where the sun got too close and burned the earth became the deserts. When the sun was too far away, the cold areas became the North and South Poles. The Greeks used many myths to explain the facts of nature.

GO

15 Helios probably let Phaethon drive the sun chariot because —

A Helios wanted a day off from his job.

B Helios' wife urged him to do it.

C Phaethon had done it before.

D the boy begged, and Helios loved him.

16 There is enough information in the story to show that —

F the ancient Greeks were foolish people.

G the Greeks used myths to explain what they did not understand.

H the Greek story was true, and we are wrong today.

J the sun was both closer to the earth and farther away many years ago.

17 Look at the web of this story.

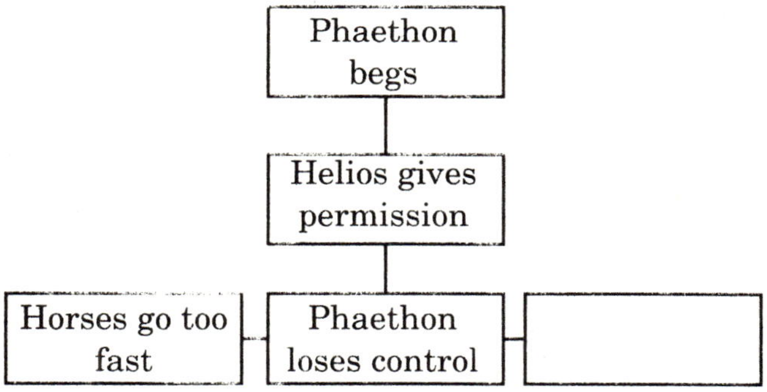

Which of these would best fit in the blank part?

A Helios sorry, Helios punished

B Chariot crashes into desert

C Sun burns and freezes earth

D Phaethon handles reins wrong

18 Which words at the end of the story show that Phaethon realized his mistake?

F "Please, Father, let me drive."

G "I wasn't strong enough to do your job."

H One day Helios finally agreed.

J Phaethon wasn't handling the reins the same as usual.

19 The author included the first paragraph in order to —

A tell about the origin of this myth.

B explain that the Greeks were not scientific.

C persuade people to believe the Greek myths.

D explain why we have seasons.

20 In order to answer number 19, the best thing to do is —

F re-read the first paragraph.

G skim the beginning of each paragraph.

H make an outline of the story.

J look for the key word "author."

21 What is another good title for this story?

A "A Wonderful Adventure"

B "The Sun and the Sky"

C "How the Ground Was Burned"

D "A Foolish Mistake"

STOP

ANSWER ROWS 15 Ⓐ Ⓑ Ⓒ Ⓓ 17 Ⓐ Ⓑ Ⓒ Ⓓ 19 Ⓐ Ⓑ Ⓒ Ⓓ 21 Ⓐ Ⓑ Ⓒ Ⓓ
16 Ⓕ Ⓖ Ⓗ Ⓙ 18 Ⓕ Ⓖ Ⓗ Ⓙ 20 Ⓕ Ⓖ Ⓗ Ⓙ

Example

Directions: Read each passage. Find the best answer to the questions that follow the passage.

E1

The puppy looked at the huge mountain. He started climbing, always keeping his eyes on the little girl at the top. Finally he reached her. She bent over the little puppy and picked him up. She said, "Good job, Markey." The little puppy had just climbed a hill about four feet high.

To the puppy, it seemed as if —

A the mountain was covered with snow.
B he was climbing a huge mountain.
C he was a big dog at last.
D the little girl was lost.

Here is a story about a girl who had an unusual experience. Read the story and then do numbers 1 through 6 on page 35.

Dragons aren't real, right? You read about them in fairy tales and see them in the movies, but they don't really exist. Well, I had an experience that changed my mind, and it might change your mind, too.

One night I was having trouble getting to sleep. I tossed and turned and bunched up my pillow, but nothing seemed to help. I was beginning to become drowsy when I heard a strange noise in the backyard. I got out of bed and looked out my window. There in the backyard was a huge dragon looking right at me! I rubbed my eyes, shook my head, and looked again. He was still there, and he was talking to me.

"Hey, Donna. I need your help. Something's happened and I can't fly."

This was too weird. A dragon in my backyard was talking to me, asking me to help him. My parents always told me not to talk to strange people, but not to strange dragons.

"Are you for real?" I asked.

"Of course I'm real," he answered. "Can't you see me standing in front of you? I'm as real as the nose on your face. Now, will you help me or not? I'm desperate. It's late and I want to go home."

"Sure. I'll help. What can I do?"

I decided that the easiest thing to do was to go with the flow. If this talking dragon was asking me to help him out, I might as well give it a try.

"Great. Just climb down that tree and jump on my back. You can look at my wings and see what's wrong."

"Just a second while I get changed."

"Okay, but please hurry. Sunrise is just a few hours away, and I don't want to end up in a circus."

I changed quickly and crawled out the window onto a huge tree limb. It took me only a minute to climb down to the ground. This wasn't the first time I'd taken the express route to the backyard.

"If you will just climb up my tail and take a look at my wings, you can tell me what's wrong with them. They've been bothering me for more than a week now."

"Hmm. I can see what the problem is. You don't seem to have any wings."

GO

"Of course I do," said the dragon. "I've had them for years."

"Let me look closer."

I crawled up the dragon's tail and looked carefully at its back. I still couldn't see any wings. The only thing I could see was a pair of flaps. I stuck my hand into the flaps and felt something that could have been folded wings.

"Are your wings folded up inside your flaps?"

"My wings are inside my flaps? That must be the problem. My wings are stuck inside my flaps. What on earth will I do?"

1 What is the "express route to the backyard?"

A Climbing down a fire escape

B Running down the back stairs

C Running down the front stairs

D Climbing down a tree

2 Why is the dragon worried about the sunrise?

F He might be captured.

G It will weaken him

H He won't be able to fly.

J The sun will damage his wings.

3 Which of these is the most likely ending for the story?

A The dragon will fly away before sunrise.

B Donna will wake up from a dream.

C Donna will introduce the dragon to her friends.

D The dragon will end up in a circus.

4 Why is the dragon having trouble flying?

F The sun has affected his wings.

G He can't see in the dark.

H His wings are stuck in his flaps.

J His tail is wrapped around his wings.

5 What does the expression "go with the flow" mean in this story?

A To climb down the tree

B To go along with what is happening

C To go with the dragon

D To go along with a practical joke

6 This story would be considered —

F biography.

G non-fiction.

H fantasy.

J science.

GO

ANSWER ROWS E1 Ⓐ Ⓑ Ⓒ Ⓓ 2 Ⓕ Ⓖ Ⓗ Ⓙ 4 Ⓕ Ⓖ Ⓗ Ⓙ 6 Ⓕ Ⓖ Ⓗ Ⓙ

1 Ⓐ Ⓑ Ⓒ Ⓓ 3 Ⓐ Ⓑ Ⓒ Ⓓ 5 Ⓐ Ⓑ Ⓒ Ⓓ

Reina hated walking home from school. Even though it was just a few blocks, it was disgusting. Trash was everywhere, graffiti was all over the walls, and junked cars lined the streets. She couldn't understand how people could live that way. It was wonderful when she got home to her neat house and yard that stood out like a picture on a dingy wall.

"Mom, was our neighborhood always so terrible?"

"Not at all, Honey. Why ten years ago, this was one of the most wonderful neighborhoods in the city. People took care of their houses and had beautiful gardens. It was so nice that people came from all over to walk through the neighborhood and look at the houses." Mrs. Chavez sighed and looked away.

"I wish it were like that now. I hate being outside. It's such a mess, it makes me feel dirty."

Mrs. Chavez thought about what Reina had said. That night, after Reina was asleep, she and her husband talked it over. They decided Reina was right, and that since the city wasn't going to do anything about the neighborhood, they would have to.

On Saturday morning, Mr. Chavez knocked on his neighbor's door. He explained his idea to Mr. Jackson, who, despite being over seventy years old, agreed to help. The Chavez family and Mr. Jackson spent the morning cleaning up the trash in the tiny "pocket park" on the corner.

About noon, some of the other neighbors came out to lend a hand, even though no one had asked them. Before they knew it, there were more than twenty people working in the park. There were so many, in fact, that some of them decided to pick up the trash on the sidewalks and in the street.

Mrs. Alioto, who lived adjacent to the park, called her son and asked him to come and pick up the trash in his truck. By Saturday afternoon, the park was spotless, and the truckload of trash they had picked up was on its way to a city landfill.

For the next few weeks, the neighbors came out each evening and tackled another job. They planted flowers, continued to pick up the trash that thoughtless people kept throwing on the ground, and convinced the city to tow the junked cars away. Little by little, the neighborhood started to look better.

Reina noticed that something else was happening, too. Some of the unpleasant people who had been hanging out on her street weren't around as much. The children in the neighborhood were also playing outside more. And she didn't mind the walk home from school at all.

GO

7 Why does Mrs. Chavez sigh and look away when Reina asks her about the neighborhood?

A She is ignoring Reina.

B She is thinking about work.

C She is thinking about another neighborhood.

D She is remembering how it used to be.

8 Which problem will the neighbors find most difficult to solve?

F Finding a way to move the trash they pick up to the landfill

G Convincing thoughtless people to stop throwing trash on the ground

H Getting started

J Planting flowers

9 In the beginning of the story, how does Reina feel about her neighborhood?

A Happy

B Excited

C Determined

D Disgusted

10 The reaction of the other neighbors to seeing the park cleaned up shows that

F they wanted to help solve the problem.

G they didn't think there was much of a problem to solve.

H they enjoyed sleeping late.

J they wanted to clean up their own yards first.

11 In the eighth paragraph, what do the words "adjacent to" mean?

A Next to

B Far from

C Across the street from

D On the next block

12 Why does the writer mention Mr. Jackson's age?

F Because it is unusual for a person to be that old

G Because he was Reina's grandfather

H Because he lived adjacent to the park

J To show that older people are willing to help clean up the neighborhood

13 What is a "pocket park"?

A A park on a corner

B A small park

C A large park

D A park with small flowers

14 What is the main point of this story?

F Young people are more likely to solve problems than old people.

G Parents should listen to their children more often.

H People sometimes have to take action to solve neighborhood problems.

J Trash is a major problem in many city neighborhoods.

GO

ANSWER ROWS
7 Ⓐ Ⓑ Ⓒ Ⓓ 9 Ⓐ Ⓑ Ⓒ Ⓓ 11 Ⓐ Ⓑ Ⓒ Ⓓ 13 Ⓐ Ⓑ Ⓒ Ⓓ
8 Ⓕ Ⓖ Ⓗ Ⓙ 10 Ⓕ Ⓖ Ⓗ Ⓙ 12 Ⓕ Ⓖ Ⓗ Ⓙ 14 Ⓕ Ⓖ Ⓗ Ⓙ

A Wise Warrior

Sequoya was a Cherokee Indian warrior who did a great service for his people. Sequoya saw that white settlers could read and write. He realized that the soldiers who got letters from home could read the squiggles and understand a message from someone far away. Reading and writing allowed information to be sent long distances and saved for the future.

The warrior knew that his own people had no way of recording things that were important. They could only tell the old stories and hope that their children listened and learned so that they could retell the stories to the next generation. If the Cherokees had a system of writing, Sequoya reasoned, people who had not yet been born could learn the old stories.

Sequoya called the soldiers' and settlers' books and papers "talking leaves." He thought the pages of paper looked like leaves. Sequoya decided to invent a system of writing for the Cherokees. It was not an easy task. He had to record symbols with charcoal on pieces of bark for each sound in the Cherokee language. Then he had to combine and reorganize these symbols into an alphabet. He had to come up with a simple system which would be easy for the people to learn to read and write. It took Sequoya many years to invent this alphabet.

When he finally took his alphabet to the tribal council, he had to convince them that it was usable. As a test, Sequoya left the room. The leaders were to tell his daughter something to write. She wrote it down, and he had to come back into the room and read the message. He was afraid that some problem would come up because the council asked her to write on paper with a quill pen. Before, she had always written on bark with a piece of charcoal. The council waited for him to read the message. He read, "The Cherokee nation shall live for all time." The council was convinced, and the group approved his plan.

Many Cherokees learned to read and write, and later, they published their own newspaper. Sequoya was a hero. All his time and effort had paid off. He was a warrior, but not in a war; by being wise, he had won the battle against ignorance.

GO

15 Sequoya spent many years writing on pieces of bark with charcoal because —

A he was trying to learn to read English.

B he was trying to make up an alphabet.

C he did not like to work or hunt.

D he did not know how to tell stories.

16 Where did Sequoya take the alphabet for approval?

F To the Cherokee tribal council

G To his family

H To the soldiers and settlers

J To the teachers in the school

17 Before Sequoya's invention, the Cherokee Indians —

A wrote on bark with charcoal.

B kept their history by word of mouth.

C read the squiggles on paper.

D didn't allow the use of writing.

18 Sequoya first learned about writing from the —

F tribal elders.

G other tribes.

H older Cherokees who told stories.

J soldiers and settlers.

19 In this article, the phrase, "the next generation" means —

A the children's children.

B other Indian tribes.

C the soldiers and settlers.

D people who can't read.

20 There is enough information in the story to show that —

F writing is the only way to send information from one generation to another.

G Sequoya learned to write at a college in the East.

H not every group of people invented writing on their own.

J English is the easiest language to use for writing the Cherokee language.

21 The article is most like —

A a biography.

B a folktale.

C a story from history.

D an adventure story.

GO

ANSWER ROWS 15 Ⓐ Ⓑ Ⓒ Ⓓ 17 Ⓐ Ⓑ Ⓒ Ⓓ 19 Ⓐ Ⓑ Ⓒ Ⓓ 21 Ⓐ Ⓑ Ⓒ Ⓓ
16 Ⓕ Ⓖ Ⓗ Ⓙ 18 Ⓕ Ⓖ Ⓗ Ⓙ 20 Ⓕ Ⓖ Ⓗ Ⓙ

LET'S CLEAN UP OUR TOWN!

The city and the environmental council are sponsoring a clean-up campaign in all neighborhoods on Saturday, October 14. Families, clubs, organizations, and individuals are invited to participate.

Prizes will be awarded in the following categories:

- **Most trash collected (bags will be weighed)**
- **Most unusual thing picked up (judges will decide)**
- **Most people participating in a group**
- **Largest area covered**

Participants must meet at the parking lot on the corner of Pickett and St. John Streets at 8:30 AM Saturday, October 14, to register. Everyone will get an orange vest, a name tag, and trash bags. There is no limit to the ages of participants. Weigh-in and judging will take place at the same location at 3:00 PM.

PRIZES

- **free movie tickets for everyone in the group**
- **food coupons from Happy Harry's Hamburger Heaven**
- **gift certificates from Ye Olde Toy Store**
- **trophies**
- **ribbons for second and third places**

All clean-up participants are invited to a cook-out and awards presentation ceremony at Pickett and St. John at 6:00 PM.

Come out and clean up!

22 Who is donating coupons as a prize?

F Ye Olde Toy Store

G Our Town Cinema movie theater

H Food Basket grocery store

J Happy Harry's Hamburger Heaven

23 Which words in the passage tell that others besides groups can participate in the clean-up?

A ...no limit to the ages...

B ...individuals are invited...

C ...come out and clean up...

D ...families, clubs, and organizations...

24 When will the prizes be awarded?

F 6:00 PM

G 8:30 AM

H 3:00 PM

J 12:00 noon

25 This announcement would probably be found in all of these places *except* —

A the window of Happy Harry's Hamburger Heaven.

B a local newspaper.

C an environmental club's newsletter.

D the Yellow Pages.

26 People who will take part in this campaign probably live in —

F this city.

G in the country or far suburbs.

H in the next state.

J in another town the same size.

27 This announcement gives you a reason to believe that —

A the city is going to make people who litter pay fines.

B someone will make lots of money by picking up trash on October 14.

C the town has a problem with trash on the streets.

D no one in this town cares enough to join in a clean-up project.

28 What other project is similar to cleaning up the town?

F Raising money for a vacation.

G Building a nicer house for the mayor.

H Painting over graffiti.

J Going to a big sale at the mall.

GO

ANSWER ROWS 22 Ⓕ Ⓖ Ⓗ Ⓙ 24 Ⓕ Ⓖ Ⓗ Ⓙ 26 Ⓕ Ⓖ Ⓗ Ⓙ 28 Ⓕ Ⓖ Ⓗ Ⓙ
23 Ⓐ Ⓑ Ⓒ Ⓓ 25 Ⓐ Ⓑ Ⓒ Ⓓ 27 Ⓐ Ⓑ Ⓒ Ⓓ

For numbers 29 through 32, choose the best answer to the question.

29 Which of these statements from a book review expresses a fact?

A Anne Price is my favorite author, and I know many others enjoy her work.

B *The Year of the Raisin* was written by Anne Price, a native of Egypt.

C It's not the best book I ever read, but *The Year of the Raisin* is clearly on my top-ten list.

D The only real problem with *The Year of the Raisin* is that the author spends too little time describing the scenery.

30 Which of these probably came from a science fiction story?

F Scientists are still not sure how the moon was formed.

G When I was young, I was fascinated by the moon, but I never expected that some day I would help to build rockets that would fly there.

H NASA reported today that the next space shot would be delayed at least one day because of the weather.

J The vessel approached the domed city that had been established on the dark side of the moon.

31 Which of these statements from a newspaper article expresses an opinion?

A The principal language in England is, of course, English, but it is spoken differently from American English.

B London is served by an extensive subway system called the Underground that circles the city.

C Automobiles in England have the steering wheel on the right, which is the opposite of American cars.

D A trip to England is inexpensive, and people generally have a good time, even when the weather is poor.

32 Most of the people in Folsom were what most of us think of as being normal. The Rayburn's, however, were not. From the house in which they lived to their hobbies, they were most unusual.

Which part of a story does this passage tell about?

F The setting

G The characters

H The plot

J The mood

STOP

ANSWER ROWS 29 Ⓐ Ⓑ Ⓒ Ⓓ 31 Ⓐ Ⓑ Ⓒ Ⓓ
30 Ⓕ Ⓖ Ⓗ Ⓙ 32 Ⓕ Ⓖ Ⓗ Ⓙ

NUMBER RIGHT ______

Name and Answer Sheet

To the Student:

These tests will give you a chance to put the tips you have learned to work.

A few last reminders…

- Be sure you understand all the directions before you begin each test. You may ask the teacher questions about the directions if you do not understand them.
- Work as quickly as you can during each test.
- When you change an answer, be sure to erase your first mark completely.
- You can guess at an answer or skip difficult items and go back to them later.
- Use the tips you have learned whenever you can.
- It is OK to be a little nervous. You may even do better.

Now that you have completed the lessons in this unit, you are on your way to scoring high!

STUDENT'S NAME

LAST	FIRST	MI
11 columns, each: ○ A B C D E F G H I J K L M N O P Q R S T U V W X Y Z	6 columns, each: ○ A B C D E F G H I J K L M N O P Q R S T U V W X Y Z	1 column: ○ A B C D E F G H I J K L M N O P Q R S T U V W X Y Z

SCHOOL

TEACHER

FEMALE ○ MALE ○

BIRTH DATE

MONTH	DAY		YEAR	
JAN ○	0	0		0
FEB ○	1	1		1
MAR ○	2	2		2
APR ○	3	3		3
MAY ○		4		4
JUN ○		5	5	5
JUL ○		6	6	6
AUG ○		7	7	7
SEP ○		8	8	8
OCT ○		9	9	9
NOV ○				
DEC ○				

GRADE

④ ⑤ ⑥

PART 1 VOCABULARY

E1 Ⓐ Ⓑ Ⓒ Ⓓ	**6** Ⓕ Ⓖ Ⓗ Ⓙ	**13** Ⓐ Ⓑ Ⓒ Ⓓ	**20** Ⓕ Ⓖ Ⓗ Ⓙ	**26** Ⓕ Ⓖ Ⓗ Ⓙ	**31** Ⓐ Ⓑ Ⓒ Ⓓ
E2 Ⓕ Ⓖ Ⓗ Ⓙ	**7** Ⓐ Ⓑ Ⓒ Ⓓ	**14** Ⓕ Ⓖ Ⓗ Ⓙ	**21** Ⓐ Ⓑ Ⓒ Ⓓ	**27** Ⓐ Ⓑ Ⓒ Ⓓ	**32** Ⓕ Ⓖ Ⓗ Ⓙ
1 Ⓐ Ⓑ Ⓒ Ⓓ	**8** Ⓕ Ⓖ Ⓗ Ⓙ	**15** Ⓐ Ⓑ Ⓒ Ⓓ	**22** Ⓕ Ⓖ Ⓗ Ⓙ	**28** Ⓕ Ⓖ Ⓗ Ⓙ	**33** Ⓐ Ⓑ Ⓒ Ⓓ
2 Ⓕ Ⓖ Ⓗ Ⓙ	**9** Ⓐ Ⓑ Ⓒ Ⓓ	**16** Ⓕ Ⓖ Ⓗ Ⓙ	**23** Ⓐ Ⓑ Ⓒ Ⓓ	**29** Ⓐ Ⓑ Ⓒ Ⓓ	**34** Ⓕ Ⓖ Ⓗ Ⓙ
3 Ⓐ Ⓑ Ⓒ Ⓓ	**10** Ⓕ Ⓖ Ⓗ Ⓙ	**17** Ⓐ Ⓑ Ⓒ Ⓓ	**24** Ⓕ Ⓖ Ⓗ Ⓙ	**30** Ⓕ Ⓖ Ⓗ Ⓙ	**35** Ⓐ Ⓑ Ⓒ Ⓓ
4 Ⓕ Ⓖ Ⓗ Ⓙ	**11** Ⓐ Ⓑ Ⓒ Ⓓ	**18** Ⓕ Ⓖ Ⓗ Ⓙ	**25** Ⓐ Ⓑ Ⓒ Ⓓ		
5 Ⓐ Ⓑ Ⓒ Ⓓ	**12** Ⓕ Ⓖ Ⓗ Ⓙ	**19** Ⓐ Ⓑ Ⓒ Ⓓ			

PART 2 READING COMPREHENSION

E1 Ⓐ Ⓑ Ⓒ Ⓓ	**5** Ⓐ Ⓑ Ⓒ Ⓓ	**10** Ⓕ Ⓖ Ⓗ Ⓙ	**15** Ⓐ Ⓑ Ⓒ Ⓓ	**20** Ⓕ Ⓖ Ⓗ Ⓙ	**25** Ⓐ Ⓑ Ⓒ Ⓓ
1 Ⓐ Ⓑ Ⓒ Ⓓ	**6** Ⓕ Ⓖ Ⓗ Ⓙ	**11** Ⓐ Ⓑ Ⓒ Ⓓ	**16** Ⓕ Ⓖ Ⓗ Ⓙ	**21** Ⓐ Ⓑ Ⓒ Ⓓ	**26** Ⓕ Ⓖ Ⓗ Ⓙ
2 Ⓕ Ⓖ Ⓗ Ⓙ	**7** Ⓐ Ⓑ Ⓒ Ⓓ	**12** Ⓕ Ⓖ Ⓗ Ⓙ	**17** Ⓐ Ⓑ Ⓒ Ⓓ	**22** Ⓕ Ⓖ Ⓗ Ⓙ	**27** Ⓐ Ⓑ Ⓒ Ⓓ
3 Ⓐ Ⓑ Ⓒ Ⓓ	**8** Ⓕ Ⓖ Ⓗ Ⓙ	**13** Ⓐ Ⓑ Ⓒ Ⓓ	**18** Ⓕ Ⓖ Ⓗ Ⓙ	**23** Ⓐ Ⓑ Ⓒ Ⓓ	**28** Ⓕ Ⓖ Ⓗ Ⓙ
4 Ⓕ Ⓖ Ⓗ Ⓙ	**9** Ⓐ Ⓑ Ⓒ Ⓓ	**14** Ⓕ Ⓖ Ⓗ Ⓙ	**19** Ⓐ Ⓑ Ⓒ Ⓓ	**24** Ⓕ Ⓖ Ⓗ Ⓙ	

Part 1 Vocabulary

Examples

Directions: Find the word or words that mean the same or almost the same as the underlined word.

E1 **pour in a funnel**

A cup without handles
B cone-shaped object
C small pot
D large pan

E2 **Which of these probably comes from the Latin word *fluere* meaning *to flow*?**

F floor
G few
H fluent
J flash

For numbers 1-8, find the word or words that mean the same or almost the same as the underlined word.

1 **walk through the mist**

A snow
B archway
C fog
D forest

2 **a colorful display**

F group of birds
G type of clothing
H drawing
J exhibit

3 **offer expired**

A began
B saved
C ended
D lasted

4 **be fortunate**

F prompt
G pleased
H honest
J lucky

5 **A barricade is a kind of—**

A door
B barrier
C journey
D statement

6 **Something that is reliable is —**

F dependable
G new
H rich
J unhappy

7 **A forecast is like a —**

A signal
B negative statement
C prediction
D positive statement

8 **To mingle is to —**

F avoid
G mix with
H separate from
J escape

9 Do you think we can trust his opinion?

Trust means —

A understand
B believe
C hear
D summarize

10 It was a gloomy day.

Gloomy means —

F bright
G cold
H dark
J damp

11 The produce we bought at the farm stand was wonderful.

Produce means —

A canned food
B bakery products
C clothing
D fruits and vegetables

12 Victor clenched his trophy.

Clenched means —

F held tightly
G carried far
H lost
J dropped

13 We will have to delay the game.

To delay is to —

A play in spite of the weather
B put off until later
C start earlier
D play harder

For numbers 14-19, find the word that means the opposite of the underlined word.

14 an awkward puppy

F graceful
G unusual
H friendly
J clumsy

15 become weary

A happy
B stronger
C busier
D tired

16 lessen the pressure

F teach
G reduce
H increase
J forget

17 ignore a warning

A quietly whisper
B loudly shout
C listen carefully to
D pay no attention to

18 exhausted runner

F refreshed
G victorious
H frustrated
J tired

19 moist soil

A soaked
B deep
C fertile
D dry

GO

For numbers 20–23, choose the word that correctly completes both sentences.

20 Randy ________ bad about the game.

We'll cover the table with ________ .

F responded
G felt
H cloth
J acted

21 The ________ of Maine is rocky.

Be careful if you ________ down the hill on your bike.

A shore
B speed
C coast
D race

22 The students ________ up for the bus.

The box is ________ with metal.

F covered
G stood
H insulated
J lined

23 Reggie wants to ________ his clothes.

All the ________ fell out of Rea's pocket.

A change
B money
C pack
D coins

24 | **This test is a major part of your grade.** |

In which sentence does the word major mean the same thing as in the sentence above?

F My grandfather was an Air Force major.

G He plays baseball in the major leagues.

H The new plant was a major discovery.

J My older brother will major in art at the state university.

25 | **The number seven can't be divided by two.** |

In which sentence does the word number mean the same thing as in the sentence above?

A The winner of the drawing is number two-hundred ten.

B Number each box, then seal it.

C The number of students who came was higher than we thought.

D A number of us are going to the beach.

For numbers 26 and 27, choose the answer that best defines the underlined part.

26 unusual unkind

F much
G almost
H not
J partly

27 respectable honorable

A lacking a characteristic
B possessing a characteristic
C somewhat
D hardly

28 Which of these words probably comes from the Latin word *terminare* meaning *to end*?

- **F** torrential
- **G** stem
- **H** return
- **J** terminate

29 Which of these words probably comes from the Middle English word *patron* meaning *a model*?

- **A** pattern
- **B** parrot
- **C** partial
- **D** attract

30 That gem is ________ valuable, so be sure to store it safely.

Which of these words means the gem has special value?

- **F** particularly
- **G** minimally
- **H** occasionally
- **J** repeatedly

31 The high water ________ all the way to the lower branches of the oak tree.

Which of these words means the high water reached to the lower branches of the oak tree?

- **A** exposed
- **B** managed
- **C** descended
- **D** extended

Read the paragraph. Find the word below the paragraph that fits best in each numbered blank.

The beads that __(32)__ clothes and jewelry today have a long history. The first beads were __(33)__ natural objects like pieces of bone, wood, or shell. Later, people learned to make beads from clay and to __(34)__ holes in stones and pieces of metal. Beads have been used to help people count and to __(35)__ business transactions, and in many societies, they served the same purpose as money. Some of the most extraordinary beadwork ever found was done by the native cultures in North and South America.

32
- **F** purchase
- **G** beneath
- **H** support
- **J** decorate

33
- **A** hardly
- **B** recently
- **C** probably
- **D** abruptly

34
- **F** fill
- **G** drill
- **H** mine
- **J** alert

35
- **A** record
- **B** cost
- **C** cancel
- **D** rely

STOP

Example **Directions:** Read the selection, then choose the best answer to the question.

E1

Officers of the First Central Bank announced yesterday that construction of the West Avenue branch will begin on March 1. If all goes according to plan, the branch office will be finished by August 15. When the new branch is completed, First Central Bank will have a total of 7 offices in town, including the central office on Powell Street. The last branch office was opened on October 8 of last year.

When will the West Avenue branch of the First Central Bank be finished?

A March 1

B October 8

C August 15

D August 7

Here is a story about a remarkable historic discovery. Read the story and then do numbers 1 through 8 on page 50.

In 1879, a group of explorers made an incredible find. They discovered paintings of remarkable beauty on the walls of a cave in Spain. Some scientists believed that these paintings were created by early humans from the Stone Age, between ten and thirty thousand years ago. Other scientists and the public did not believe the claim, but over the years, it was proven correct. Our ancestors had incredible artistic talents.

Most of the cave art that has been discovered has been found in Spain and France. A smaller number of such caves are located in Italy, Portugal, Russia, and other countries. Scientists believe that many more caves will be discovered in the coming years, and are concentrating their efforts on Africa and the area between Europe and Asia. These two regions of the world were populated first by humans.

Cave art was carved or painted on the walls and roofs of caves, usually near the entrance. The entrance area was probably chosen to take advantage of daylight and to allow many people to view the paintings. In some cases, the art appears much deeper in caves and requires artificial light. Evidence suggests that the artists used torches or shallow bowls in which animal fat was burned.

Primitive artists were able to create with a wide variety of colors, including yellow, red, brown, green, and black. These colors came from minerals that were ground and mixed with animal fat, vegetable juice, water, or even blood. The colors were applied with sticks or brushes made of animal hair. One of the most unusual means of applying color was to blow it through a hollow reed.

The most popular subject of cave art was animals. They included mammoths, horses, deer, bison, cave lions, wild cattle, and wooly rhinoceros. Many of the animals shown in cave paintings are now extinct. Scientists are not sure why early humans made cave paintings, but some of the paintings appear to show successful hunts, while others might have been intended to bring good luck during upcoming hunts. Other popular subjects include human figures, battles, and surprisingly, human hands. The outlines of human hands have been found on every continent where humans created cave art.

1 What was the response of the general public to the discovery of cave art made by Stone Age people?

A They believed it at first.

B They did not believe it.

C They thought it was beautiful.

D They ignored it.

2 From cave paintings, scientists learned that —

F Stone Age people thought caves were sacred places.

G animals were not hunted for food during the Stone Age.

H some animals that are extinct now were alive during the Stone Age.

J the temperature was much warmer during the Stone Age.

3 Based on the passage, what can you conclude about animal fat?

A It does not burn.

B Stone Age artists used it to preserve their paintings.

C It can be burned to produce light.

D Stone Age artists mixed it with their food.

4 Where do scientists expect to find more cave paintings?

F In Central and South America

G In Spain and France

H In places where there are caves with large openings

J In regions of the world first populated by humans

5 In the fourth paragraph, what does the word "primitive" mean?

A European or African

B Talented

C Untalented

D Early in history

6 Paintings that were created deep inside caves —

F could be viewed easily by daylight.

G were always made using the juice from plants.

H were probably seen by fewer people than paintings near the entrance.

J usually show more animals than paintings near the entrance.

7 What can you conclude about minerals?

A Primitive humans knew how to turn minerals into metal.

B Different types of minerals can be used to make different kinds of colors.

C Different types of minerals were used to represent different animals.

D The minerals used for paintings were always found in caves.

8 Where would this passage be most likely to appear?

F In a textbook about early human history

G In a textbook about modern art

H In a dictionary

J In an encyclopedia entry about caves

GO

In this story, a cowgirl finds herself lost in a sudden storm. She finds her way into a canyon that shelters her from the storm. Read the story, then do numbers 9 through 14.

Mystery Canyon

"New Year's Eve is one heck of a time to freeze to death," Rose muttered to herself. She scrunched down into her duster and tried to warm up, but it was pretty much hopeless. She wished she were back at home with the kids and Grandpa, but she had a job to do. This herd of cows was a year's worth of mortgage, and she wasn't about to lose a single head.

When she had started out that morning, it was a New Mexico blue sky day. At about noon she had caught up with her herd of beefers and was heading them back to the pasture near the house. The sky by then was leaden, and by one o'clock, the snow had started to fall. Within an hour, the storm had turned real nasty, and she couldn't see fifty yards in front of her. She had finally given up and was looking for a tree, a large rock, anything that might give them shelter from the wind and snow.

"This isn't the worst, Chico. Remember that sandstorm last summer? I had to tie my bandannas over your nose and mouth, but you still got us home with your eyes closed. I know you'll get us out of this jam."

Her voice was calm and encouraging, and Chico responded by pushing a little harder through the snow. The cows were still with them, but they were clearly tiring. Rose knew they wouldn't last much longer without a rest. She was worried, but was a long way from panic. Somebody once said about Rose that a brick would panic before she did, and they were right. She'd been through some terrible times on the range, and this was just one more thing she'd deal with.

Chico continued to trudge on, and the steers did their best to stay up with the strong, young horse. Within fifteen minutes, however, Rose knew it was hopeless to go on, and she and Chico rounded the herd into a tight group. With some luck, they might all survive the night.

Knowing how dangerous it would be to fall asleep, Rose struggled to stay awake, when the tinkling of bells jolted her back to consciousness. For a moment she thought she was imagining the sound, then it happened again. Chico and the steers must have heard it, for their ears perked up and they all turned in the same direction. As if on cue, Chico and the herd started moving toward the sound.

In a few minutes, Chico had led them to a narrow canyon. It's towering walls blocked the wind, and the small stream flowing through it seemed to warm the air slightly. Chico sniffed the air for an instant and then headed confidently into the canyon.

The canyon broadened slightly as they continued into it and a few trees showed themselves through the storm. A little farther along Rose discovered the source of the tinkling. A small cabin nestled at the end of the canyon, and on the porch, a harness hung from nails. With each gust of wind, the bells on the harness dropped a handful of notes.

Chico walked to the cabin as if it were a home he had always known. The cows moved into the pasture and started grazing on the tufts of grass that reached through the snow. Even Rose felt a tingling warmth, the same feeling she had known as a little girl when she rushed into her grandmother's kitchen after a long, cold ride home from school.

The front door of the cabin opened and a head stuck out. "Take your horse into the barn. You can unsaddle in there and give him some hay and water. Then come on in the back door. It's too awful out there for an old man to be more neighborly."

Rose took care of Chico and trudged over to the cabin. Before she stepped inside, she saw a few deer had joined her cows in the pasture. A row of mountain bluebirds lined the fence around the pasture, and in the cottonwoods by the stream sat a pair of owls who watched her every move. The yellow eyes of several coyotes sparked in the deeper parts of the canyon, but they seemed so tame that she didn't think they posed any threat to the herd.

"Quite a bunch of critters out there," Rose said as she walked through the door. "I guess this storm has made buddies of all the locals. My name's Rose, and I'm sure glad to meet you."

"I'm Sandy, or at least that's what they call me, although my hair's not been that color for a longer time than I can remember." His white hair was gathered into a ponytail that hung down the back of his flannel shirt. "The ponytail's not a fashion statement. I just don't get to the barber very often, and well, this is pretty easy to take care of. Can I get you something warm? Here, sit down by the fire."

"Anything warm would be great," sighed Rose, "and I'd love to sit down by that fire."

"You're the Shipley girl, aren't you?" Sandy asked as he handed her a cup of tea. "Your folks have been around here for quite a spell. How's the family?"

"Grandmother died a few years ago. Grandpa's living with me and the kids now. How long have you lived here? I didn't know there was a ranch or even a canyon back here."

"It's easy to miss, and I kind of like my privacy. If you ride below the ridge you can't see the opening, and not many folks have any reason to climb the ridge."

9 By the end of the passage, the feelings of the girl have changed from —

A trust → joy

B respect → anger

C excitement → disappointment

D concern → comfort

GO

10 Rose was most concerned about losing the cows because they were a "year's worth of mortgage." Which of these means about the same as a *year's worth of mortgage*?

F Money needed for a family vacation this year

G Money needed to pay for the house for a year

H A long period of time without money

J Something worth more than she would earn in a year

11 The relationship between Rose and her horse Chico is most like —

A two friends who have worked together a long time.

B a stranger helping out a person she just met.

C a boy making a new student in the class feel comfortable.

D an experienced doctor knowing what to do when someone is hurt.

12 How does the author describe the sound of the bells?

F A noise that frightened Chico and the cows

G Coyotes howling deep in the canyon among the trees

H Notes being dropped

J As loud as the wind that was howling around Rose and Chico

13 What is the most important thing the author wants you to know about the canyon?

A The stream in the canyon kept the air warm.

B There was a barn in the canyon that Rose could use for Chico.

C In the canyon, animals were friendlier than they were in other places.

D It was hidden and Rose didn't know about it.

14 Which of these ideas suggests the canyon is more special than it first appears?

F The cows ate the grass in the canyon, even though it was snowing hard and was windy.

G Rose and Chico felt comfortable in the canyon, even though they had never been there before.

H Birds were sitting on the fence.

J The walls of the canyon blocked the wind.

Here is a passage about an important part of every plant. Read the story and then do numbers 15 through 17.

The roots of trees, shrubs, and other plants perform two major functions. Roots keep the plant upright in the same place, and they feed the plant by absorbing moisture and nutrients from the soil.

Different plants have different kinds of roots. The roots of some plants go deep into the soil, while others spread out sideways for great distances. You might be surprised to learn that the giant redwoods of California have relatively shallow roots. This is because they grow in the mountains where there is very little soil. The shallow roots allow the trees to absorb as much moisture as possible. Unfortunately, a strong wind can blow a redwood tree down much more easily than other, smaller trees with deeper roots.

If you look closely at small roots, you will see that they are delicate. Don't be fooled by their appearance. Tiny roots can work their way into the smallest spaces and can crack the hardest stones. When roots have established themselves well in the soil, it is almost impossible to remove the plant without damaging it.

The roots of all plants share several common characteristics. One is geotropism, the tendency to grow down into the earth. In other words, roots follow the pull of gravity. If you plant a seed upside down and watch it grow, you will notice that the young root will emerge from the top of the seed and then turn immediately down.

A second characteristic is hydrotropism. Roots have a tendency to grow in the direction of water. If the source of water is deep in the soil, the roots will grow down. If the source of water is near the surface, the roots will grow sideways. Hydrotropism can be a problem for home owners who landscape with certain plants. Willow trees, for example, love moisture, and will send their roots in the direction of the nearest source of water. Near a house, this is often underground water or sewer pipes, which will become clogged with tree roots.

A third characteristic roots share is the ability to regenerate the plant. Under certain conditions, a tiny piece of root can be nurtured so it grows into a new plant. The process of regeneration happens sometimes in nature with hardy species like dandelions and bamboo. In the highly controlled environment of a laboratory or greenhouse, almost every plant can be regenerated from a healthy piece of root.

Roots are not usually considered to be an attractive part of a plant. In some Asian countries, however, the roots of trees may be trained to grow above ground into exotic shapes. This is especially true with bonsai plants, miniature versions of full-sized plants. The process of training the roots and the other parts of the plant is painstaking and takes many years.

15 According to the passage, geotropism is the tendency for roots to —

A grow downward in response to gravity.

B grow downward in response to moisture.

C grow upward in response to gravity.

D grow upward in response to moisture.

16 Which of these would be the best title for the passage?

F "How Roots Grow"

G "Tropism"

H "Shallow and Deep Roots"

J "Remarkable Roots"

17 Desert plants often have large but shallow root systems. This is probably because —

A the principal source of moisture is underground springs.

B the principal source of moisture is occasional rain.

C there is less gravity in the desert.

D there is more gravity in the desert.

GO

Finding Our Heritage

Historic Pleasanton, the city's history and heritage council, is sponsoring a contest for young people's organizations. Clubs such as Scouts, church groups, and even neighborhood groups are encouraged to participate. Prizes will be awarded in each age group. The council will provide money for eligible projects entered in the contest.

If you would like to enter, send a letter with the following information:

1. Your plan for exploring our history or heritage. Describe the purpose of the project, what you intend to do, and how you will let the public know what you found. (Newspaper article, booklet, computer program, video, etc.)
2. The cost of your project. List items that must be bought and their prices.
3. The number of people in your group.
4. The age of the people in your group.
5. The names of the adult sponsors, their addresses and their telephone numbers.
6. The date you hope to begin and the length of time this project will take.

Plans must be submitted no later than May 31. Projects must be completed by September 1.

For more information, call Julia Happyhands, 214-555-5432. Send letters to:
Historic Pleasanton
1234 Good Street
Pleasanton, Texas 75432

The adult sponsors will be notified if the group is chosen. Projects will be judged when they are completed. Winners will also be honored at the Pleasanton Fall Festival in October. Winning groups will ride on floats in the Fall Festival Parade.

18 **Groups who wish to enter the contest should first —**

F get the money to pay for their project.

G start working on their project.

H write a letter to the council.

J call Ms. Happyhands

19 **Projects that will be considered for prizes must —**

A be entered by young people's organizations.

B investigate how the United States grew from a colony to a real country.

C deal with solving today's problems.

D focus on creating more jobs in the town.

20 **The heritage contest announcement might be posted in all of these places *except* a —**

F local newspaper.

G message board at Pleasanton City Hall.

H bulletin boards at local shopping malls.

J newspaper ad in a city 100 miles away.

21 **These directions were written in order to —**

A tell how to do a good deed.

B offer money for making Pleasanton more popular.

C get people to ride on floats in the parade.

D present guidelines for entering the contest.

22 **Which of these groups would *not* be eligible for the contest?**

F Adults working for a business in Pleasanton

G A Girl Scout troop of 10-year-olds

H Three families of children aged 5 to 15

J A summer camp class of 12-year-olds at the YMCA

23 **The purpose of sending the letter to the council is to —**

A let people know what the name of your group is.

B help the council decide on a name for the contest.

C show that a group can actually complete a project.

D get more information from the council.

24 **Groups who are winners will receive —**

F materials for their projects.

G prizes and honors at the Fall Festival.

H blue ribbons for each participant.

J a money prize of $100.

GO

For numbers 25 through 28, choose the best answer to the question.

25 Which of these probably came from the beginning of a book about young people who solve a mystery?

A The young people gathered in Wilson Park and waited quietly. They expected the spring to begin flowing again any minute, if all went well.

B Wilson Park was named after Jasper Wilson, a merchant who opened the first grocery in Lansdale soon after the town was founded.

C For more than 200 years, a spring had fed the pond at the edge of Wilson Park. Last year, for some unknown reason, the spring simply stopped flowing.

D As they climbed the cliff, Jennie and Roberto could hear the sound of water, but no matter how hard they looked, they couldn't see it.

26 Which of these statements from an encyclopedia expresses a fact?

F Mozart is recognized as being the greatest composer in history.

G Because of technology, there are more ways to enjoy music than ever before.

H The finest music was composed during the seventeenth and eighteenth centuries.

J Musicians today are less talented than those of twenty years ago.

27 The crowd at the beach was having a wonderful time. The sky was clear, the sun was bright, and the ocean temperature was almost perfect.

What part of a story does this passage tell about?

A The plot

B The characters

C The mood

D The setting

28 Which of these statements probably came from a true story about the natural world?

F The fall migration of sandhill cranes begins in northern Canada and ends many thousands of miles away in Texas or New Mexico.

G The hawks looked at one another, nodded their heads, and agreed the cliff would make a wonderful home for them and their chicks.

H "I'm too dull," the mallard thought. "I could use more colorful feathers."

J The geese laughed at the fox who had fallen into the pond and was very unhappy.

STOP

Table of Contents
Language

Lesson 1 Punctuation

Examples

Directions: Mark the space for the punctuation mark that is needed in the sentence. Mark the space for "None" if no more punctuation marks are needed.

A Yes I remembered to lock the door.

A . **B** , **C** " **D** None

B The pilot said, "We should land in about an hour."

F ? **G** " **H** . **J** None

Tips

Read the sentence word by word. Look carefully for missing punctuation marks.

Stay with your first answer choice. You should change an answer only if you are sure the first one you chose is incorrect.

Practice

1 Watch out for the poison ivy

A ! **B** ? **C** . **D** None

2 The parking lot was filled with cars trucks, and motorcycles.

F : **G** " **H** , **J** None

3 How can I help you

A ! **B** . **C** ? **D** None

4 It will be sunny this afternoon," answered Emily.

F , **G** " **H** : **J** None

5 Someone forgot to put the trash out.

A , **B** ! **C** ? **D** None

6 No Randy can't go swimming with you.

F , **G** . **H** ; **J** None

GO

ANSWER ROWS
A Ⓐ Ⓑ Ⓒ Ⓓ 1 Ⓐ Ⓑ Ⓒ Ⓓ 3 Ⓐ Ⓑ Ⓒ Ⓓ 5 Ⓐ Ⓑ Ⓒ Ⓓ
B Ⓕ Ⓖ Ⓗ Ⓙ 2 Ⓕ Ⓖ Ⓗ Ⓙ 4 Ⓕ Ⓖ Ⓗ Ⓙ 6 Ⓕ Ⓖ Ⓗ Ⓙ

For numbers 7-12, read each answer. Fill in the space for the choice that has a punctuation error. If there is no mistake, fill in the fourth answer space.

7 **A** Why did the bus
B pass by without stopping
C Now we will be late.
D *(No mistakes)*

8 **F** The bank will be
G closed on Monday
H because of the holiday.
J *(No mistakes)*

9 **A** Your books pencils
B and paper are on the table.
C Lunch is in the refrigerator.
D *(No mistakes)*

10 **F** 64 North Street
G Parker OH, 32187
H June 7, 1995
J *(No mistakes)*

11 **A** Dear Diana
B Thanks for the hat you sent me.
C It is really outrageous.
D *(No mistakes)*

12 **F** Say hello to your family for me.
G Your friend,
H Ahmad
J *(No mistakes)*

For numbers 13-16, read each sentence with a blank. Choose the word or words that fit best in the blank and show the correct punctuation.

13 Our ________ playground is one of the best in town.

A schools
B schools'
C schools's
D school's

14 We gave ________ a present for his birthday.

F Mr. Winston, our mail carrier
G Mr. Winston, our mail carrier,
H Mr. Winston our mail carrier
J Mr. Winston, our mail, carrier

15 The cat is sleeping on the ________ the dog is eating.

A bed, and
B bed, and,
C bed and,
D bed and

16 Juanita ________ tell us what the surprise was.

F wouldnt
G wouldnt'
H wouldn't
J would'nt

STOP

ANSWER ROWS
7 Ⓐ Ⓑ Ⓒ Ⓓ 9 Ⓐ Ⓑ Ⓒ Ⓓ 11 Ⓐ Ⓑ Ⓒ Ⓓ 13 Ⓐ Ⓑ Ⓒ Ⓓ 15 Ⓐ Ⓑ Ⓒ Ⓓ
8 Ⓕ Ⓖ Ⓗ Ⓙ 10 Ⓕ Ⓖ Ⓗ Ⓙ 12 Ⓕ Ⓖ Ⓗ Ⓙ 14 Ⓕ Ⓖ Ⓗ Ⓙ 16 Ⓕ Ⓖ Ⓗ Ⓙ

Examples

Directions: Mark the space for the answer that shows correct punctuation and capitalization. Mark the space for “Correct as it is” if the underlined part is correct.

A
- **A** We ate lunch at Irma’s house.
- **B** We were so hungry we cleaned our plates’ quickly.
- **C** Her Father cook’s well.
- **D** After lunch we played game’s.

B How do you know which way to go?
- **F** way, to go?
- **G** way to go!
- **H** way to go.
- **J** Correct as it is

Tips

Look carefully at all the answer choices before you choose the one you think is correct.

Remember, you are looking for the answer that shows correct capitalization and punctuation.

Practice

1
- **A** “Let’s go for a walk suggested Willa.”
- **B** Alonzo added quickly, we can hike up Sandy Peak.”
- **C** “This tree,” said Francisco, “is over a hundred years old.”
- **D** “What kind of tree is it.” Elinor asked?

2
- **F** Our trip began in Chicago illinois
- **G** We spent a few days hiking near Jackson, Wyoming.
- **H** In Yellowstone, National, Park we saw bears and elk.
- **J** We went through beautiful scenery on our way to Denver colorado.

3
- **A** Glass has been used to make many, surprising things.
- **B** Two of the most unusual, are walking canes and pipes.
- **C** The most common use of glass. Is for windows?
- **D** Thin glass is easily broken, but thick glass is very strong.

4 It is so late that the hardware store is probably closed.
- **F** probably closed?
- **G** probably, closed.
- **H** probably closed!
- **J** Correct as it is

5 The museum is on king street and the restaurant is about a block away.
- **A** King Street, and
- **B** King Street and,
- **C** king street, and
- **D** Correct as it is

6 “Who was on the phone?” wondered Lydia?
- **F** Lydia.”
- **G** Lydia!
- **H** Lydia.
- **J** Correct as it is

GO

ANSWER ROWS				
	A Ⓐ Ⓑ Ⓒ Ⓓ	1 Ⓐ Ⓑ Ⓒ Ⓓ	3 Ⓐ Ⓑ Ⓒ Ⓓ	5 Ⓐ Ⓑ Ⓒ Ⓓ
	B Ⓕ Ⓖ Ⓗ Ⓙ	2 Ⓕ Ⓖ Ⓗ Ⓙ	4 Ⓕ Ⓖ Ⓗ Ⓙ	6 Ⓕ Ⓖ Ⓗ Ⓙ

(7) Owls are unusual <u>birds they</u> hunt at night and rest in a
(8) protected spot during the day. An <u>owl's eyes</u> can't move, so to look around, an owl must move its head almost in a full circle. The
(9) foods that owls enjoy include <u>insects small animals, and</u> even fish.
(10) Owls are found all over the <u>World?</u>

7 A birds? They
B birds, they
C birds. They
D Correct as it is

8 F owls eyes
G owls' eyes
H owls eye's
J Correct as it is

9 A insects, small animals, and,
B insects, small animals, and
C insects, small, animals, and,
D Correct as it is

10 F world.
G world?
H World.
J Correct as it is

October 10, 1995

Central Computer Company
PO Box 548
(11) <u>Ridd, Utah</u> 84651
(12) <u>Dear Ms. Walton</u>

Please send me your catalog. I am interested in buying
(13) software for my <u>computer and</u> my friends say yours is the best.

(14) <u>Sincerely Yours</u>
Jane Gibbons

11 A Ridd Utah
B Ridd Utah,
C Ridd, Utah,
D Correct as it is

12 F dear Ms. Walton:
G Dear Ms. Walton:
H Dear ms. Walton;
J Correct as it is

13 A computer, and
B computer. And
C computer and,
D Correct as it is

14 F sincerely yours
G Sincerely Yours:
H Sincerely yours,
J Correct as it is

GO

ANSWER ROWS 7 Ⓐ Ⓑ Ⓒ Ⓓ 9 Ⓐ Ⓑ Ⓒ Ⓓ 11 Ⓐ Ⓑ Ⓒ Ⓓ 13 Ⓐ Ⓑ Ⓒ Ⓓ
8 Ⓕ Ⓖ Ⓗ Ⓙ 10 Ⓕ Ⓖ Ⓗ Ⓙ 12 Ⓕ Ⓖ Ⓗ Ⓙ 14 Ⓕ Ⓖ Ⓗ Ⓙ

For numbers 15 and 16, read the sentence with a blank. Mark the space beside the answer choice that fits best in the blank and has correct capitalization and punctuation.

15 We visited the office of ________ when we were in Washington.

A senator margaret fowler
B Senator Margaret Fowler
C senator Margaret Fowler
D Senator Margaret fowler

16 The taxi driver ________ would you like to go?"

F asked, "Where
G asked "Where
H asked. Where
J "Asked where

Julia wrote this report about the traffic in her neighborhood. Read the report and use it to do numbers 17-20.

People in our neighborhood have complained (1) about traffic for a long time. I decided to see how (2) bad it really was. What I found surprised me from (3) monday through friday more than 40 cars a minute cross Miller Street between 7:00 and 9:00 in the morning. The same is true between 4:00 and 6:00 in (4) the afternoon. From 9:00 and 6:00, however, the (5) Average Traffic is only 12 cars per minute.

17 In sentence 1, neighborhood have is best written —

A neighborhood. Have
B neighborhood have,
C Neighborhood have
D As it is

18 In sentence 2, me from is best written -

F me, from
G Me from
H me. From
J As it is

19 In sentence 3, monday through friday is best written —

A Monday ,through Friday
B Monday through Friday.
C Monday through Friday
D As it is

20 In sentence 5, Average Traffic is best written —

F average traffic
G Average Traffic,
H Average, Traffic
J As it is

STOP

ANSWER ROWS 15 Ⓐ Ⓑ Ⓒ Ⓓ 17 Ⓐ Ⓑ Ⓒ Ⓓ 19 Ⓐ Ⓑ Ⓒ Ⓓ
16 Ⓕ Ⓖ Ⓗ Ⓙ 18 Ⓕ Ⓖ Ⓗ Ⓙ 20 Ⓕ Ⓖ Ⓗ Ⓙ

Example

Directions: Fill in the space for the choice that has a punctuation error. If there is no mistake, fill in the fourth answer space.

E1

How did you finish the job so quickly?

A . **B** ! **C** : **D** None

1 "Your stop, warned the conductor, "is coming up soon."

A " **B** ; **C** ? **D** None

2 Don't bump into that cactus

F ? **G** . **H** ! **J** None

3 Yes, this shirt is on sale today.

A : **B** , **C** ; **D** None

4 Did you ever wonder who built that house

F . **G** ? **H** : **J** None

For numbers 5-7, read each answer. Fill in the space for the choice that has a punctuation error. If there is no mistake, fill in the fourth answer space.

5 **A** We werent able
B to go to the picnic
C at the lake last Sunday.
D *(No mistakes)*

6 **F** Cindy will have to leave by six.
G It is the only way she will
H get there on time?
J *(No mistakes)*

7 **A** Does Dad still have to wash
B the dishes glasses and pots
C from last night's party?
D *(No mistakes)*

For numbers 8 and 9, read each sentence with a blank. Choose the word or words that fit best in the blank and show the correct punctuation.

8 The book was ________ the movie was even better.

F good but,
G good. But
H good, but,
J good, but

9 No matter how hard we tried, we couldn't move the ________.

A log's
B logs
C logs'
D logs's

GO

ANSWER ROWS E1 Ⓐ Ⓑ Ⓒ Ⓓ 2 Ⓕ Ⓖ Ⓗ Ⓙ 4 Ⓕ Ⓖ Ⓗ Ⓙ 6 Ⓕ Ⓖ Ⓗ Ⓙ 8 Ⓕ Ⓖ Ⓗ Ⓙ
1 Ⓐ Ⓑ Ⓒ Ⓓ 3 Ⓐ Ⓑ Ⓒ Ⓓ 5 Ⓐ Ⓑ Ⓒ Ⓓ 7 Ⓐ Ⓑ Ⓒ Ⓓ 9 Ⓐ Ⓑ Ⓒ Ⓓ

For numbers 10-13, read each group of sentences. Find the one that is written correctly and shows the correct capitalization and punctuation.

10 **F** Let's rake up the leaves before we mow the lawn,

G The lawn mower is in the shed?

H Did you know that the garage door is open?

J The Shovel and Rake aren't where you said they would be.

11 **A** Miami Florida, is visited by many tourists from other Countries.

B If you visit london, England, be sure to ride the subway.

C The oldest zoo in the United States is in Philadelphia, Pennsylvania.

D The sacramento river provides water to many farms in California.

12 **F** I was late for the bus, but everyone else was on time.

G Rita and Andrew, arrived yesterday.

H The bags are packed, and are in the trunk of the car.

J A vacation is fun but, only if you plan it right.

13 **A** Obed reminded Anne, "That she promised to help."

B We should buy some trees and plant them in the park," suggested Lillian.

C "The city council has given us permission, added Clifford.

D "Did you remember to bring your money?" asked Billie.

For numbers 14-17, read the sentence with a blank. Mark the space beside the answer choice that fits best in the blank and has correct capitalization and punctuation.

14 The store at 209 Mill ________ is closed for renovations.

F St
G St.
H ST
J ST.

15 We ________ walk too close to the edge of the cliff.

A shouldn't
B shouldnt'
C Shouldnt
D should'nt

16 ________ is learning how to build furniture in wood shop.

F Sondra my cousin
G Sondra my cousin,
H Sondra, my cousin,
J Sondra my Cousin

17 The only state Mrs. Sullivan hasn't visited is ________

A alaska.
B alaska,
C Alaska?
D Alaska.

GO

ANSWER ROWS 10 Ⓕ Ⓖ Ⓗ Ⓙ 12 Ⓕ Ⓖ Ⓗ Ⓙ 14 Ⓕ Ⓖ Ⓗ Ⓙ 16 Ⓕ Ⓖ Ⓗ Ⓙ
11 Ⓐ Ⓑ Ⓒ Ⓓ 13 Ⓐ Ⓑ Ⓒ Ⓓ 15 Ⓐ Ⓑ Ⓒ Ⓓ 17 Ⓐ Ⓑ Ⓒ Ⓓ

For numbers 18-21, look at the underlined part of each sentence. Find the answer choice that shows the correct capitalization and punctuation for the underlined part.

18 I am sure that shes going to find a job that pays well.

- **F** she's
- **G** shes'
- **H** She's
- **J** Correct as it is

19 Ray is learning about the lakes, rivers, and swamps in our county.

- **A** lakes rivers and
- **B** lakes. Rivers and
- **C** lakes, rivers, and,
- **D** Correct as it is

20 "How did Cora know where the kitten was hiding." Wondered Jacob.

- **F** hiding?" Wondered
- **G** hiding," Wondered
- **H** hiding?" wondered
- **J** Correct as it is

21 The driver tried to stop but the car skidded on the wet road.

- **A** stop. But
- **B** stop, but
- **C** stop but,
- **D** Correct as it is

For numbers 22-25, read the passage. Find the answer choice that shows the correct capitalization and punctuation for the underlined part.

A river gives life to the land it passes through. The water of a
(22) river supports fish frogs and birds that depend on it for food and shelter. Plants thrive along a river because of the moisture it
(23) provides and many animals prefer to live near rivers because of the abundant plants and prey there. Since the dawn of history,
(24) humans have chosen to live near rivers whenever they could. Great
(25) cities like paris and cairo were founded near rivers.

22
- **F** fish; frogs, and
- **G** Fish frogs and
- **H** fish, frogs, and
- **J** Correct as it is

23
- **A** provides, and
- **B** provides and.
- **C** provides. And
- **D** Correct as it is

24
- **F** humans'
- **G** human's
- **H** humans's
- **J** Correct as it is

25
- **A** Paris and Cairo,
- **B** Paris and Cairo
- **C** paris. And Cairo
- **D** Correct as it is

GO

ANSWER ROWS 18 Ⓕ Ⓖ Ⓗ Ⓙ 20 Ⓕ Ⓖ Ⓗ Ⓙ 22 Ⓕ Ⓖ Ⓗ Ⓙ 24 Ⓕ Ⓖ Ⓗ Ⓙ
19 Ⓐ Ⓑ Ⓒ Ⓓ 21 Ⓐ Ⓑ Ⓒ Ⓓ 23 Ⓐ Ⓑ Ⓒ Ⓓ 25 Ⓐ Ⓑ Ⓒ Ⓓ

This is more of Julia's report about traffic. Read the report and use it to do numbers 26-29.

(1) I discovered that the biggest problem with traffic in our neighborhood is that it is heavy only during two periods of the day. (2) How can we solve the problem. (3) The easiest way is to ask people to change the time they go to work and return home. (4) Many businesses in Los angeles and other cities are letting people do this today. (5) It is called flex time. (6) Although workers' schedules are flexible, they still put in the same number of hours each week. (7) People who are on flex time like it and seem to work harder. (8) Changing the time they begin and end work allows people more time to do things like sports shopping and chores. (9) Some experts believe that flex time will become even more popular in the future because people will value their time more.

26 In sentence 2, problem. is best written —

- **F** problem?
- **G** problem!
- **H** problem:
- **J** As it is

27 In sentence 4, Los angeles is best written —

- **A** los angeles
- **B** los Angeles
- **C** Los Angeles
- **D** As it is

28 In sentence 6, workers' is best written —

- **F** workers
- **G** worker's
- **H** Workers
- **J** As it is

29 In sentence 8, sports shopping and is best written —

- **A** sports, shopping and,
- **B** sports, shopping, and
- **C** sports, shopping, and,
- **D** As it is

STOP

ANSWER ROWS 26 Ⓕ Ⓖ Ⓗ Ⓙ 27 Ⓐ Ⓑ Ⓒ Ⓓ 28 Ⓕ Ⓖ Ⓗ Ⓙ 29 Ⓐ Ⓑ Ⓒ Ⓓ NUMBER RIGHT ______

Lesson 4 Usage

Examples

Directions: Read the directions for each section. Fill in the circle for the answer you think is correct.

A Randy's parents ________ a new car because the old one was in an accident.

A buyed
B bought
C buying
D did bought

B

F Where the nearest supermarket?
G Items in a supermarket so similar things are together.
H Our family goes food shopping about once a week.
J It takes us about an hour. To buy everything we need.

Tips

If you are not sure which answer is correct, try each one in the blank. Choose the one that sounds the best.

If you are not sure which answer is correct, take your best guess.

Practice

For numbers 1-3, choose the word or phrase that best completes the sentence.

1 Lena hurt ________ climbing a tree.

A itself
B themselves
C she
D herself

2 He is ________ in history than I am.

F interested
G interesting
H most interested
J more interested

3 Sid ________ in a marathon next week.

A ran
B will run
C was running
D to run

For numbers 4-6, choose the answer that is a complete and correctly written sentence.

4

F They want to climb to the top of the Plaza Building.
G Each week us does something different in the city.
H Remind they that the museum has a special program for children.
J Her said she will meet us down town.

5

A The directions didn't make any sense.
B Theo didn't want to waste no time putting the shelves together.
C We ain't never going to finish!
D Kami can't find the bolts nowhere.

6

F The corn grew tallest than the beans.
G Marilyn grew the most tastiest peas.
H It is too early to plant a garden.
J Good tools are more expensiver.

GO

ANSWER ROWS

A Ⓐ Ⓑ Ⓒ Ⓓ 1 Ⓐ Ⓑ Ⓒ Ⓓ 3 Ⓐ Ⓑ Ⓒ Ⓓ 5 Ⓐ Ⓑ Ⓒ Ⓓ

B Ⓕ Ⓖ Ⓗ Ⓙ 2 Ⓕ Ⓖ Ⓗ Ⓙ 4 Ⓕ Ⓖ Ⓗ Ⓙ 6 Ⓕ Ⓖ Ⓗ Ⓙ

For numbers 7-12, read each answer choice. Fill in the space for the choice that has a usage error. If there is no mistake, fill in the fourth answer space.

7 **A** A open door is not
B a good reason to walk
C into a house without knocking.
D *(No mistakes)*

8 **F** There are a few
G kinds of athletic shoes
H that are still on sale.
J *(No mistakes)*

9 **A** A large flock of
B gooses landed in the
C river near our school.
D *(No mistakes)*

10 **F** The car it got a flat
G tire on our way home
H from the soccer game.
J *(No mistakes)*

11 **A** The photographer called
B to tell us that the
C class pictures was finished.
D *(No mistakes)*

12 **F** When did you decide
G that you wanted
H to become a doctor?
J *(No mistakes)*

For numbers 13 and 14, choose the best way to write the underlined part of each sentence. If the underlined part is correct, fill in the fourth answer space.

13 **<u>Before</u>** the weather is good, we should paint the outside of the house.

A Although
B While
C After
D *(No change)*

14 The apple trees around the pond **<u>was covered</u>** with blossoms.

F to cover
G covering
H were covered
J *(No change)*

For numbers 15 and 16, choose the answer that is a complete and correctly written sentence.

15 **A** The open window the cat jumped to the ground.
B Cleaning the driveway with a large broom.
C Caroline and Willard on their way to the amusement park.
D We were surprised by the size of the package.

16 **F** The mail on the table, the magazines in a rack nearby.
G You can come with us, but be sure to tell your mother where you are going.
H A truck turned the corner, and too fast so the driver had to stop quickly.
J Watching the news on television, talking about it with my mother.

GO

ANSWER ROWS
7 Ⓐ Ⓑ Ⓒ Ⓓ 9 Ⓐ Ⓑ Ⓒ Ⓓ 11 Ⓐ Ⓑ Ⓒ Ⓓ 13 Ⓐ Ⓑ Ⓒ Ⓓ 15 Ⓐ Ⓑ Ⓒ Ⓓ
8 Ⓕ Ⓖ Ⓗ Ⓙ 10 Ⓕ Ⓖ Ⓗ Ⓙ 12 Ⓕ Ⓖ Ⓗ Ⓙ 14 Ⓕ Ⓖ Ⓗ Ⓙ 16 Ⓕ Ⓖ Ⓗ Ⓙ

William wrote this story about a trip he took to Canada. Read the story and use it to do numbers 17-20.

(1) When I found out that I was invited to join my aunt and uncle on a fishing vacation to Canada, I will be excited. (2) The trip proved to be even more fabulous than I thought.

(3) The trip began with a longest drive to a small town north of the city of Winnipeg. (4) We were headed toward a lake, and I thought that was where we were going to fish. (5) We drove up to a plane that was floating in the lake and parked beside a dock. (6) My aunt and uncle got out and spoke to a woman working near the boat. (7) Then them came back and asked me to start unloading the car. (8) They said the woman, an expert pilot, was going to fly us to the lake where we would stay in a lodge for a week.

17 In sentence 1, will be excited is best written —

- **A** was exciting
- **B** was excited
- **C** were excited
- **D** As it is

18 In sentence 3, a longest drive is best written —

- **F** a long drive
- **G** a longer drive
- **H** a most long drive
- **J** As it is

19 In sentence 7, them came is best written —

- **A** their came
- **B** they comes
- **C** they came
- **D** As it is

20 In sentence 8, expert pilot is best written —

- **F** expertest pilot
- **G** expertly pilot
- **H** more expert pilor
- **J** As it is

STOP

ANSWER ROWS 17 Ⓐ Ⓑ Ⓒ Ⓓ 18 Ⓕ Ⓖ Ⓗ Ⓙ 19 Ⓐ Ⓑ Ⓒ Ⓓ 20 Ⓕ Ⓖ Ⓗ Ⓙ

Examples

Directions: Read the directions for each section. Fill in the circle for the answer you think is correct.

Find the underlined part that is the simple subject of the sentence.

A A can fell from the shelf in the store.
A (can) B (fell) C (shelf) D (store)

Find the underlined part that is the simple predicate (verb) of the sentence.

B Farad jumped over the small creek.
F (Farad) G (jumped) H (small) J (creek)

Choose the answer that best combines the underlined sentences.

C The window is locked.
The door is locked.

A The door is locked also with the window.
B The door and window is locked.
C The window is locked, and the door.
D The window and door are locked.

Tips

If a question is too difficult, skip it and come back to it later.

If you are not sure which answer choice is correct, say each one to yourself. The right answer usually sounds best.

Practice

For numbers 1-3, find the underlined part that is the simple subject of the sentence.

1 The coins fell through a hole in my pocket.
A (coins) B (through) C (hole) D (pocket)

2 A group of hunters found the injured farmer.
F (group) G (hunters) H (found) J (farmer)

3 Last month, my cousin won a tennis tournament.
A (Last) B (month) C (cousin) D (tennis)

For numbers 4-6, find the underlined part that is the simple predicate (verb) of the sentence.

4 The huge crane lifted the logs from the barge.
F (huge) G (lifted) H (logs) J (barge)

5 Lenny usually arrives at the office before eight o'clock.
A (Lenny) B (usually) C (arrives) D (office)

6 Stars twinkled brightly in the night sky.
F (Stars) G (twinkled) H (brightly) J (night)

GO

ANSWER ROWS
A Ⓐ Ⓑ Ⓒ Ⓓ   C Ⓐ Ⓑ Ⓒ Ⓓ   2 Ⓕ Ⓖ Ⓗ Ⓙ   4 Ⓕ Ⓖ Ⓗ Ⓙ   6 Ⓕ Ⓖ Ⓗ Ⓙ
B Ⓕ Ⓖ Ⓗ Ⓙ   1 Ⓐ Ⓑ Ⓒ Ⓓ   3 Ⓐ Ⓑ Ⓒ Ⓓ   5 Ⓐ Ⓑ Ⓒ Ⓓ

For numbers 7-9, choose the answer that best combines the underlined sentences.

7 The television is plugged in.

The television still isn't working.

A If the television is plugged in, it still won't work.

B The television still isn't working because it is plugged in.

C Because the television is still plugged in, it isn't working.

D The television is plugged in, but it still isn't working.

8 We fixed the roof yesterday.

The roof was damaged by the storm.

F Yesterday, we fixed the roof that was damaged by the storm.

G The roof was damaged by the storm yesterday, so we fixed it.

H The roof, which we fixed yesterday, and was damaged by the storm.

J Damaged by the storm, we fixed the roof yesterday.

9 My grandmother still enjoys hiking.

My grandmother is almost seventy.

My grandmother also enjoys fishing.

A Hiking and fishing, my grandmother is almost seventy.

B My grandmother is almost seventy, but she enjoys hiking, and she enjoys fishing.

C My grandmother, who is almost seventy, still enjoys hiking and fishing.

D Because she is almost seventy, my grandmother enjoys hiking and fishing.

For numbers 10 and 11, choose the best way of expressing the idea.

10 **F** Although clear in the morning, it began forming clouds in the afternoon.
G In the morning it was clear, but clouds began forming in the afternoon.
H Clouds began forming in the afternoon, and it was clear in the morning.
J It was clear in the morning, because clouds began forming in the afternoon.

11 **A** Before you come home, pick up the paper, but check the mailbox.
B Pick up the paper, then check the mailbox, then come home.
C Pick up the paper and check the mailbox before you come home.
D Although you come home, pick up the paper and check the mailbox.

GO

ANSWER ROWS 7 Ⓐ Ⓑ Ⓒ Ⓓ 8 Ⓕ Ⓖ Ⓗ Ⓙ 9 Ⓐ Ⓑ Ⓒ Ⓓ 10 Ⓕ Ⓖ Ⓗ Ⓙ 11 Ⓐ Ⓑ Ⓒ Ⓓ

Here is more of William's story about his trip to Canada. Use the story to do numbers 12-15.

We all got in the plane and fastened our seat belts. **(1)** The pilot started the engines. **(2)** She signaled a worker on the dock and told him to untie several ropes. **(3)** The plane moved slowly away from the dock, and the pilot gradually increased the speed of the motor. **(4)** We began moving faster and soon lifted off the lake. **(5)** The plane made a graceful turn, and then the plane headed north. **(6)**

For a while we flew over pretty land. **(7)** Below us were rivers, lakes, and huge forests. **(8)** We could see herds of deer and elk, and every once in a while, another plane or a boat on a lake. **(9)** There were no towns at all, and I knew we were heading into the deep wilderness. **(10)**

12 How is sentence 1 best written?

- **F** Getting in the plane, while we fastened our seat belts.
- **G** Our seat belts were fastened, and we all got in the plane.
- **H** Fastening our seat belts, we got in the plane.
- **J** As it is

13 How would sentences 2 and 3 best be combined without changing their meaning?

- **A** Starting the engines and signaling a worker on the dock to untie several ropes.
- **B** She signaled a worker on the dock, and after telling him, untied several ropes.
- **C** The pilot started the engines and signaled a worker on the dock to untie several ropes.
- **D** Starting the engines, she signaled, but a worker on the dock untied several ropes.

14 Sentence 6 is best written —

- **F** The plane made a graceful turn then headed north.
- **G** Turning gracefully, then the plane headed north.
- **H** The plane headed north, and gracefully it turned.
- **J** As it is

15 What is the most colorful way to write sentence 7?

- **A** For some time we flew over land that was pretty.
- **B** For the next several hours we flew over incredible scenery.
- **C** Flying over scenery took hours.
- **D** As it is

STOP

ANSWER ROWS 12 Ⓕ Ⓖ Ⓗ Ⓙ 13 Ⓐ Ⓑ Ⓒ Ⓓ 14 Ⓕ Ⓖ Ⓗ Ⓙ 15 Ⓐ Ⓑ Ⓒ Ⓓ

Lesson 6 Paragraphs

Example

Directions: Read the directions for each section. Fill in the circle for the answer you think is correct.

Read the paragraph below. Find the best topic sentence for the paragraph.

A _______________ . All of us must eat, and most of what we eat is grown in the soil. Fruits, vegetables, and grains all need fertile soil. In addition, animals that provide us with meat and dairy products are fed grain from the rich soil of the Midwest.

A Dirt is formed through erosion and the decay of plants and animals.

B One of our most important natural resources is plain, old dirt.

C During the Ice Age, glaciers moved soil from Canada to the United States.

D Several places around the world are blessed with fertile soil.

Tips

Remember, a paragraph should focus on one idea. The correct answer is the one that fits best with the rest of the paragraph.

If you are not sure which answer is correct, eliminate answers you know are wrong and then take your best guess.

Practice

Read the paragraph below. Find the best topic sentence for the paragraph.

1 _______________ . Most people think about hiking in the mountains or other rural areas. You can, however, enjoy hiking in a city, in the suburbs, or even on the beach.

A The most important thing you need to enjoy hiking is a good pair of shoes.

B Hikes can last from a few hours to many days.

C The most famous hiking trail in the United States is the Appalachian Trail.

D Hiking is a sport you can enjoy almost anywhere.

Find the answer choice that best develops the topic sentence below.

2 Pluto is the most mysterious planet.

F It was discovered in 1930 by the astronomer Clyde Tombaugh. Pluto appears to have a single moon, named Charon.

G It is a small planet, with a diameter about one-fourth the size of the earth's. A year on Pluto is equal to more than 247 earth years.

H It is billions of miles from earth, so it is difficult to observe. Pluto also has an unusual orbit that is very different from that of the other planets.

J Before it was discovered, mathematicians calculated where Pluto should be. The astronomer Clyde Tombaugh found it almost exactly where it was supposed to be!

GO

ANSWER ROW **A** Ⓐ Ⓑ Ⓒ Ⓓ **1** Ⓐ Ⓑ Ⓒ Ⓓ **2** Ⓕ Ⓖ Ⓗ Ⓙ

For numbers 3 and 4, read the paragraph. Find the sentence that does not belong in the paragraph.

3 1. Tiny but powerful computers are found in the most unusual places. 2. Scientists use computers to perform calculations that would be almost impossible if they had to be done by hand. 3. Every new car, for example, has a computer that controls how the motor runs. 4. The heating system in many new homes is also controlled by a computer.

A Sentence 1

B Sentence 2

C Sentence 3

D Sentence 4

4 1. It takes less than six hours for a package to go from New York to California. 2. Overnight package delivery has grown into an important service for many businesses. 3. Because of overnight service, restaurants far from the ocean can serve fresh fish. 4. The millions of people who work at home depend on overnight service to send and receive their packages.

F Sentence 1

G Sentence 2

H Sentence 3

J Sentence 4

For numbers 5 and 6, read the paragraph. Find the sentence that best fits the blank in the paragraph.

5 When the vacant lot on the corner was sold, Lee Ann and her friends thought they were losing a place to play. ________________ . The company that bought the lot put a playground on the roof of their parking structure. Now Lee Ann and her friends have an even better place to play.

A They had cleaned up the lot and used it for soccer and baseball.

B The lot had been vacant for many years.

C They discovered that they were in for a pleasant surprise.

D She was a good student and captain of the basketball team.

6 The stock market is not really as mysterious as most people think. When you buy stock in a company, you own a very small part of the company. ________________. Many people invest in the stock market so they can save money for retirement.

F Another way to save is to put money in a savings account in a bank.

G If the company is successful, you will make more money than you invested.

H A person who buys and sells stock is called a stockbroker.

J Many newspapers list how much the stocks of companies are worth.

GO

For numbers 7-9, use the paragraph below to answer the questions.

> [1]Adding a new room is one of the most popular home improvements. [2]Another favorite improvement is increasing the size of the kitchen. [3]This is a good idea because families spend so much time in the kitchen. [4]For the outside of a house, building a deck is the number one improvement. [5]A deck is usually made of specially treated wood that can stand up to all kinds of weather.

7 Choose the best first sentence for this paragraph.

A Buying a new home can be expensive.
B When you add a room, it is usually one the whole family can use.
C Families often outgrow their house.
D Many people make improvements to an old home rather than buying a new one.

8 Which sentence should be left out of this paragraph?

F Sentence 1
G Sentence 3
H Sentence 4
J Sentence 5

9 Choose the best last sentence for this paragraph.

A Banks make special loans for people to improve their homes.
B Putting in a swimming pool is not as good an idea as it sounds.
C Improving a home increases its value and makes it a better place to live.
D Many people choose to make their home improvements themselves.

10 Which of the following would be most appropriate in a letter asking a company to exchange a bicycle helmet that doesn't fit?

F Please send me a new bicycle helmet. The one I received yesterday doesn't fit. I always use a bicycle helmet when I ride because I try to be safe. It is important that you send me a new one as soon as possible. My old one doesn't work very well.

G Yesterday I received the bicycle helmet I ordered from you. When I tried it on, I found it didn't fit. I checked the size and noticed that it was large rather than medium, which I ordered. I am returning the helmet and would like you to replace it with one that is medium-sized.

H The bicycle helmet I ordered from you arrived yesterday morning. I ordered it last week because my old one doesn't work well. The one you sent me doesn't fit. In order for a helmet to work, it must fit perfectly. I am returning the helmet and would like you to send me a new one.

J Everyone should wear a helmet when they ride a bicycle. I ordered one from you last week and it arrived yesterday. When I tried it on, I discovered it didn't fit. Now I won't be able to ride my bicycle. I hope you will send me another one that fits better.

GO

ANSWER ROWS 7 Ⓐ Ⓑ Ⓒ Ⓓ 8 Ⓕ Ⓖ Ⓗ Ⓙ 9 Ⓐ Ⓑ Ⓒ Ⓓ 10 Ⓕ Ⓖ Ⓗ Ⓙ

Here is more of William's story about his trip to Canada. Use the story to do numbers 11-14.

(1) It wasn't long before the pilot slowed the engines and brought us in for a landing. **(2)** There were a bunch of things we had to do before we could start fishing. **(3)** We unloaded the plane and put everything on the dock. **(4)** The dock was about thirty feet long and six feet wide. **(5)** The pilot then took us to the cabin and showed us where everything was. **(6)** She also spent about fifteen minutes teaching us how to use the emergency radio. **(7)** We would be staying here alone, but we had to check in with a nearby ranger station twice each day. **(8)** The pilot then showed us how to start the motor on the boat and where the fishing equipment was stored. **(9)** After she was sure we were comfortable, she said good-bye and took off.

11 Which sentence could be added before sentence 6?

- **A** The cabin was surrounded by trees.
- **B** She wore regular clothes and special pilot's sunglasses.
- **C** There was no television in the cabin.
- **D** Even though it was made of logs, the cabin was large and comfortable.

12 What is the topic sentence of this paragraph?

- **F** 1
- **G** 2
- **H** 3
- **J** 4

13 What supporting information could be added after sentence 9?

- **A** The plane was white so it could be seen easily from a distance.
- **B** My uncle had done this before.
- **C** My aunt and I had eaten earlier.
- **D** The pilot said she would return for us in seven days.

14 Which sentence contains information that does *not* belong in the story?

- **F** 1
- **G** 3
- **H** 4
- **J** 7

STOP

Example

Directions: Find the underlined part that is the simple subject of the sentence.

E1

Two old trees stood beside the river.
(A: Two, B: trees, C: stood, D: river)

For number 1, choose the word or phrase that best completes the sentence.

1 The jeweler used the ________ screw I have ever seen to fix my watch.

A tiniest

B tiny

C most tiniest

D tinier

For number 2, choose the answer that is a complete and correctly written sentence.

2 **F** How did you know me and Eric were going uptown?

G Tell they to wait for us at the front door of the museum.

H She didn't hurt himself when she tripped on the chair.

J She and I ran more than three miles after school yesterday.

For numbers 3-5, read each answer choice. Fill in the space for the choice that has a usage error. If there is no mistake, fill in the fourth answer space.

3 **A** Sonia shouldn't
B have to buy no magazines
C if she doesn't want to.
D *(No mistakes)*

4 **F** The stores in town closes
G on Saturday at six o'clock, so
H we should leave by three.
J *(No mistakes)*

5 **A** You can take the bus
B from City Hall
C to the train station.
D *(No mistakes)*

For number 6, find the underlined part that is the simple subject of the sentence.

6 Your horse's saddle got wet in the storm.
(F: Your, G: horse's, H: saddle, J: storm)

For number 7, find the underlined part that is the simple predicate (verb) of the sentence.

7 The captain slowly steered the boat away from the dock.
(A: captain, B: slowly, C: steered, D: boat)

GO

ANSWER ROWS E1 Ⓐ Ⓑ Ⓒ Ⓓ 2 Ⓕ Ⓖ Ⓗ Ⓙ 4 Ⓕ Ⓖ Ⓗ Ⓙ 6 Ⓕ Ⓖ Ⓗ Ⓙ
1 Ⓐ Ⓑ Ⓒ Ⓓ 3 Ⓐ Ⓑ Ⓒ Ⓓ 5 Ⓐ Ⓑ Ⓒ Ⓓ 7 Ⓐ Ⓑ Ⓒ Ⓓ

For numbers 8-10, choose the answer that best combines the underlined sentences.

8 Roberto mowed the lawn yesterday.

The lawn looks nice.

F The nice lawn, which was mowed by Roberto yesterday.

G The lawn looks nice because Roberto mowed it yesterday.

H The lawn looks nice, and Roberto mowed it yesterday.

J The lawn, which looks nice, and Roberto mowed it yesterday.

9 The path up the mountain was steep.

The path up the mountain was slippery.

A The path up the mountain was steep and slippery.

B The path, which was steep, was slippery up the mountain.

C Up the mountain, the path was steep and slippery.

D The steep and slippery path, which went up the mountain.

10 Our town recycles aluminum.

Our town recycles glass.

Our town does not recycle plastic.

F Our town recycles aluminum, recycles glass, and does not recycle plastic.

G Aluminum and glass are recycled by our town, but our town does not recycle plastic.

H Recycling aluminum and glass, our town does not recycle plastic.

J Our town recycles aluminum and glass, but not plastic.

For numbers 11 and 12, choose the best way of expressing the idea.

11 A After the game, a party was held at a restaurant we all went to.
B We went to a party after the game, which was at a restaurant.
C We went to a restaurant, where we had a party, which was after the game.
D After the game, we all went to a restaurant for a party.

12 F Driving to the state park, it took us more than four hours.
G From home to the state park, the drive took us more than four hours.
H It took us more than four hours to drive from home to the state park.
J More than four hours, it took us to drive from home to the state park.

GO

ANSWER ROWS 8 Ⓕ Ⓖ Ⓗ Ⓙ 9 Ⓐ Ⓑ Ⓒ Ⓓ 10 Ⓕ Ⓖ Ⓗ Ⓙ 11 Ⓐ Ⓑ Ⓒ Ⓓ 12 Ⓕ Ⓖ Ⓗ Ⓙ

Read the paragraph below. Find the best topic sentence for the paragraph.

13 _______________ . Be sure you have all the ingredients you need before you start. Do all your slicing, chopping, and other preparation before you start cooking. Finally, clean up while you are cooking so there isn't a huge mess when you are finished.

A Learning to cook can be a lot of fun.

B Preparing a large meal is easier if you follow these steps.

C It is a lot of fun to serve a large meal to friends and family.

D More and more people are learning to serve healthful meals.

Find the answer choice that best develops the topic sentence.

14 The continental divide is a curious line that divides the country into two parts.

F You can't actually see the continental divide. Near some roads, however, signs point out where it is.

G The continental divide is found in the Rocky Mountain states. Some of the Rocky Mountains are over fourteen thousand feet high.

H East of the line, rivers and streams flow into the Atlantic Ocean or Gulf of Mexico. West of the divide, rivers and streams flow into the Pacific.

J The largest river east of the continental divide is the Mississippi. It begins near Canada and eventually reaches the Gulf of Mexico.

Read the paragraph below. Find the sentence that does not belong in the paragraph.

15 1. When Minnie came home after school, she was very surprised. 2. Her parents had bought new furniture. 3. It was beautiful and made the whole apartment look new. 4. They had lived in the apartment for five years and liked it very much.

A Sentence 1

B Sentence 2

C Sentence 3

D Sentence 4

Read the paragraph below. Find the sentence that best fits the blank in the paragraph.

16 India has a long and interesting history. _______________. Since then, invaders from many countries helped India develop a rich culture. India gained its independence from Britain in 1947 and became fully independent in 1950.

F Scientists believe that civilization was established in India more than 5,000 years ago.

G The population of India is expected to reach one billion within a few years.

H India is sometimes called "The World's Largest Democracy."

J The Taj Mahal, considered by some to be the most beautiful building in the world, is in India.

GO

ANSWER ROW 13 Ⓐ Ⓑ Ⓒ Ⓓ 14 Ⓕ Ⓖ Ⓗ Ⓙ 15 Ⓐ Ⓑ Ⓒ Ⓓ 16 Ⓕ Ⓖ Ⓗ Ⓙ

Below is more of William's story about his trip to Canada with his aunt and uncle. Read the story and use it to do numbers 17-20.

(1) The next morning I was awakened by the smell of breakfast cooking. **(2)** After we ate and cleaned up, we got our fishing gear and headed to the boat. **(3)** It was stored in a little house that looked like a garage on the water. **(4)** We loaded the gear into the boat, checked everything, and put our flotation vests on. **(5)** My aunt started the boat, and we headed to the far end of the lake.

(6) I have to admit that I was so excited I could hardly tie my lure on. **(7)** My aunt and uncle laughing at me fumbling with the knot. **(8)** I finally got it tied and was ready to catch a big one. **(9)** I <u>was giving</u> the honor of the first cast. **(10)** As soon as my lure hit the water, there was a huge splash. **(11)** I had hooked a fish on my first cast!

17 Which sentence could be added after sentence 1?

- **A** I don't usually get up quickly, but today I did.
- **B** Breakfast is the most important meal.
- **C** My uncle usually does the cooking.
- **D** My aunt is always reminding me to eat healthful meals.

18 How is sentence 3 best written?

- **F** Like a garage on the water, it was stored in a little house.
- **G** It was stored in a little house, and it looked like a garage on the water.
- **H** It was stored in a little house, looking like a garage on the water.
- **J** As it is

19 Which group of words is not a complete thought?

- **A** 2
- **B** 4
- **C** 7
- **D** 9

20 In sentence 9, <u>was giving</u> is best written —

- **F** would give
- **G** was given
- **H** gave
- **J** As it is

STOP

ANSWER ROWS 17 Ⓐ Ⓑ Ⓒ Ⓓ 18 Ⓕ Ⓖ Ⓗ Ⓙ 19 Ⓐ Ⓑ Ⓒ Ⓓ 20 Ⓕ Ⓖ Ⓗ Ⓙ NUMBER RIGHT ______

Lesson 8 Spelling Skills

Examples

Directions: Follow the directions for each section. Choose the answer you think is correct.

Find the word that is spelled correctly and fits best in the blank.

A She was ________ after the race.

- **A** weary
- **B** weery
- **C** wery
- **D** wiery

Choose the phrase in which the underlined word is not spelled correctly.

B
- **F** large reward
- **G** brief statement
- **H** fishing expert
- **J** favorit meal

Tips

Read the directions carefully. Be sure you know if you should look for the correctly spelled word or the incorrectly spelled word.

If you know which answer is correct, mark it and move on to the next item.

Practice

For numbers 1-5, find the word that is spelled correctly and fits best in the blank.

1 Can you ________ Roland won the contest?

- **A** beleive
- **B** beleeve
- **C** believe
- **D** beleve

2 They were ________ to a party.

- **F** invitted
- **G** invited
- **H** inveited
- **J** invyted

3 Lifting weights will increase your ________ .

- **A** strenth
- **B** strength
- **C** stringth
- **D** strinth

4 Can you solve the math ________ ?

- **F** problem
- **G** probelem
- **H** prolblem
- **J** prolbem

5 Ramon was ________ about his ability.

- **A** confidint
- **B** confedent
- **C** confedint
- **D** confident

For numbers 6-8, read the phrases. Choose the phrase in which the underlined word is not spelled correctly.

6
- **F** feel horrible
- **G** toward the house
- **H** great victorie
- **J** good customer

7
- **A** annoing sound
- **B** painful injury
- **C** tasty meal
- **D** large container

8
- **F** recognize her
- **G** old photograph
- **H** strong breeze
- **J** middle ainitial

GO

ANSWER ROWS
A Ⓐ Ⓑ Ⓒ Ⓓ 1 Ⓐ Ⓑ Ⓒ Ⓓ 3 Ⓐ Ⓑ Ⓒ Ⓓ 5 Ⓐ Ⓑ Ⓒ Ⓓ 7 Ⓐ Ⓑ Ⓒ Ⓓ
B Ⓕ Ⓖ Ⓗ Ⓙ 2 Ⓕ Ⓖ Ⓗ Ⓙ 4 Ⓕ Ⓖ Ⓗ Ⓙ 6 Ⓕ Ⓖ Ⓗ Ⓙ 8 Ⓕ Ⓖ Ⓗ Ⓙ

For numbers 9-11, read each answer. Fill in the space for the choice that has a spelling error. If there is no mistake, fill in the last answer space.

9 **A** thirsty
B classify
C messige
D multiply
E *(No mistakes)*

10 **F** wonder
G doubt
H reliabel
J prefer
K *(No mistakes)*

11 **A** second
B accident
C harbor
D listener
E *(No mistakes)*

For numbers 12-14, read each phrase. One of the underlined words is not spelled correctly for the way it is used in the phrase. Fill in the space for the word that is not spelled correctly.

12 **F** slide on ice
G cut the bored
H small portion
J beautiful island

13 **A** lesson the pain
B assist a friend
C inspect a car
D receive a notice

14 **F** bounce a ball
G great success
H good habit
J heel a wound

For numbers 15-18, find the underlined part that is misspelled. If all the words are spelled correctly, mark the space under No mistake.

15 Our garden (**A**) is similiar (**B**) to the one you visited yesterday (**C**). No mistake (**D**).

16 If you are hungary (**F**), there are snacks (**G**) in the refrigerator (**H**). No mistake (**J**).

17 Emily attended (**A**) the party disguised (**B**) as a dragon (**C**). No mistake (**D**).

18 Do you think we ought (**F**) to reveiw (**G**) our notes before taking (**H**) the test? No mistake (**J**).

STOP

ANSWER ROWS
9 A B C D E 11 A B C D E 13 A B C D E 15 A B C D E 17 A B C D E
10 F G H J K 12 F G H J K 14 F G H J K 16 F G H J K 18 F G H J K

Lesson 9 Test Yourself

Examples

Directions: For E1, find the word that is spelled correctly and fits best in the blank. For E2, choose the phrase in which the underlined word is <u>not</u> spelled correctly.

E1

The band marched in ________ .

A firmation
B formashun
C formation
D formeighten

E2

F <u>stirred</u> the soup

G short <u>anser</u>

H <u>gradual</u> change

J good <u>directions</u>

For numbers 1-6, find the word that is spelled correctly and fits best in the blank.

1 ________ the edge of the canyon slowly.

A Aproach
B Approche
C Aproche
D Approach

2 The ________ helped save the town.

F solders
G soldiers
H soldirs
J soldeirs

3 The loan will ________ him to buy a house.

A enabel
B enable
C enabell
D enabllle

4 That is an ________ flower.

F unusual
G unnusual
H unussual
J unusuall

5 Where are the ________ for the computer?

A insturections
B instrections
C instructions
D enstructions

6 Did you ________ what tools you will need?

F determin
G determine
H determen
J ditirmine

For numbers 7-10, read the phrases. Choose the phrase in which the underlined word is <u>not</u> spelled correctly.

7 **A** <u>convinsed</u> us

B <u>standard</u> size

C good <u>exercise</u>

D act <u>friendly</u>

8 **F** hard <u>question</u>

G <u>business</u> office

H small <u>nation</u>

J <u>desirve</u> the award

9 **A** <u>musical</u> instrument

B wonderful <u>bakery</u>

C the right <u>mixdure</u>

D <u>judge</u> a contest

10 **F** <u>label</u> a package

G huge <u>building</u>

H perfect <u>location</u>

J feel <u>terribel</u>

GO

ANSWER ROWS

E1	Ⓐ Ⓑ Ⓒ Ⓓ	2	Ⓕ Ⓖ Ⓗ Ⓙ	5	Ⓐ Ⓑ Ⓒ Ⓓ	8	Ⓕ Ⓖ Ⓗ Ⓙ
E2	Ⓕ Ⓖ Ⓗ Ⓙ	3	Ⓐ Ⓑ Ⓒ Ⓓ	6	Ⓕ Ⓖ Ⓗ Ⓙ	9	Ⓐ Ⓑ Ⓒ Ⓓ
1	Ⓐ Ⓑ Ⓒ Ⓓ	4	Ⓕ Ⓖ Ⓗ Ⓙ	7	Ⓐ Ⓑ Ⓒ Ⓓ	10	Ⓕ Ⓖ Ⓗ Ⓙ

For numbers 11-13, read each answer. Fill in the space for the choice that has a spelling error. If there is no mistake, fill in the last answer space.

11
A product
B wrestle
C danger
D ordinary
E *(No mistakes)*

12
F sandwhich
G abilities
H funnel
J noisy
K *(No mistakes)*

13
A sudden
B complete
C lengethy
D rarely
E *(No mistakes)*

For numbers 14-16, read each phrase. One of the underlined words is not spelled correctly for the way it is used in the phrase. Fill in the space for the word that is not spelled correctly.

14
F rough weather
G grind wheat
H great courage
J course sandpaper

15
A worst player
B peace of paper
C feel a draft
D insert a coin

16
F climb stares
G become aware
H tour guide
J number of things

For numbers 17-20, find the underlined part that is misspelled. If all the words are spelled correctly, mark the space under No mistake.

17 Mr. Desmond is oposed (A) to building (B) the new highway (C). No mistake. (D)

18 A pitcher (F) of juice (G) is in the refrigerator (H). No mistake. (J)

19 Sandy discovered (A) an old barrell (B) beside the bridge (C). No mistake. (D)

20 Doing well in school (F) will require (G) a great effert (H). No mistake. (J)

STOP

ANSWER ROWS
11 Ⓐ Ⓑ Ⓒ Ⓓ Ⓔ 14 Ⓕ Ⓖ Ⓗ Ⓙ Ⓚ 17 Ⓐ Ⓑ Ⓒ Ⓓ Ⓔ 19 Ⓐ Ⓑ Ⓒ Ⓓ Ⓔ
12 Ⓕ Ⓖ Ⓗ Ⓙ Ⓚ 15 Ⓐ Ⓑ Ⓒ Ⓓ Ⓔ 18 Ⓕ Ⓖ Ⓗ Ⓙ Ⓚ 20 Ⓕ Ⓖ Ⓗ Ⓙ Ⓚ
13 Ⓐ Ⓑ Ⓒ Ⓓ Ⓔ 16 Ⓕ Ⓖ Ⓗ Ⓙ Ⓚ

NUMBER RIGHT ______

Lesson 10 Study Skills

Example

Directions: Follow the directions for each section. Choose the answer you think is correct.

Trees
- I. Types
  - A. Evergreen
  - B. Deciduous
- II. Parts of a Tree
  - A. ________
  - B. Bark

A Line II.A. in the outline on the left is blank. Which of these fits best in the blank?

A Soil
B Forests
C Oak
D Leaves

Tips

After you have chosen the answer you think is correct, ask yourself: "Does this make sense?"

Practice

Use the Table of Contents and Index below to answer numbers 1-3.

Table of Contents

Chapter		Page
1	The History of Trains	1
2	Types of Trains	25
3	Trains and Commerce	42
4	Famous Trains	60
5	Train Travel Today	78

Index

engines
- fuel, 32–36
- types of, 30–38

history
- in Africa, 18–22
- in Asia, 20–24
- in Europe, 2–10
- in North America, 8–18
- in South America, 16–18

legends and stories, 72–78

tracks
- laying, 26–32
- types, 28–33, 93–95

workers
- job classifications, 80–85
- unions, 4–8

1 Look at the Table of Contents. Which chapter might tell how trains help farmers get their food to market?

A 1
B 2
C 3
D 4

2 Look at the Index. Which pages would probably tell about a Ghost Train some people say they have seen?

F 72–78
G 32–36
H 80–85
J 28–33

3 Look at the Table of Contents. Which of these might you find in Chapter 1?

A the differences between passenger and freight trains
B the time when and place where the railroad across the U.S. was completed
C information about the high-speed trains found in Europe and Japan
D the cost of a train ticket from Boston to Los Angeles

ANSWER ROWS **A** Ⓐ Ⓑ Ⓒ Ⓓ **1** Ⓐ Ⓑ Ⓒ Ⓓ **2** Ⓕ Ⓖ Ⓗ Ⓙ **3** Ⓐ Ⓑ Ⓒ Ⓓ

Wanda is writing a report about the future uses of computers, telephones, and television. Keep this purpose in mind when you do numbers 4-6.

4 Which of these would Wanda *not* want to include in her report?

F ways that people will use television to improve their education
G how telephones will allow more people to work at home
H the ways in which computers and televisions can be connected
J a description of the newest kitchen appliances

5 In doing her report, Wanda used the book titled *Technology Tomorrow*. Where in the book should Wanda look to learn what information is found in each chapter?

A the index
B the table of contents
C the title page
D the introduction

For number 6, read the sentence. Then choose the key words Wanda should include in her notes about technology.

6 In the coming years, telephones, televisions, and computers will become much more powerful and they will serve many of the same purposes.

F telephones, televisions, and computers made by same companies
G same methods used to make telephones, televisions, and computers
H telephones, televisions, and computers to be more powerful and more similar
J more powerful computers will replace televisions and computers

For numbers 7-9, choose the word that would appear first if the words were arranged in alphabetical order.

7 **A** feature
B female
C feel
D fern

8 **F** sister
G simple
H size
J sincere

9 **A** fine
B finger
C finish
D final

For numbers 10 and 11, choose the best source of information.

10 Which of these would tell you how to pronounce the word *soufflé*?

F an atlas
G a dictionary
H an encyclopedia
J a book of quotations

11 Which of these would help you plan the most healthful meals?

A a free cookbook from a company that sells cake mix
B an encyclopedia
C a biology book
D a book on nutrition from the U.S. government

STOP

ANSWER ROWS
4 Ⓕ Ⓖ Ⓗ Ⓙ   6 Ⓕ Ⓖ Ⓗ Ⓙ   8 Ⓕ Ⓖ Ⓗ Ⓙ   10 Ⓕ Ⓖ Ⓗ Ⓙ
5 Ⓐ Ⓑ Ⓒ Ⓓ   7 Ⓐ Ⓑ Ⓒ Ⓓ   9 Ⓐ Ⓑ Ⓒ Ⓓ   11 Ⓐ Ⓑ Ⓒ Ⓓ

Examples

Directions: Read each question, then choose the answer you think is correct.

E1

What would you find in a glossary?

A author information
B the number of chapters in a book
C publisher information
D word meanings

E2

Which of these books is a biography?

F *The History of Science*
G *Camping for Young People*
H *The Life and Times of Lincoln*
J *Music in Early America*

Study the map below. Use it to do numbers 1 and 2.

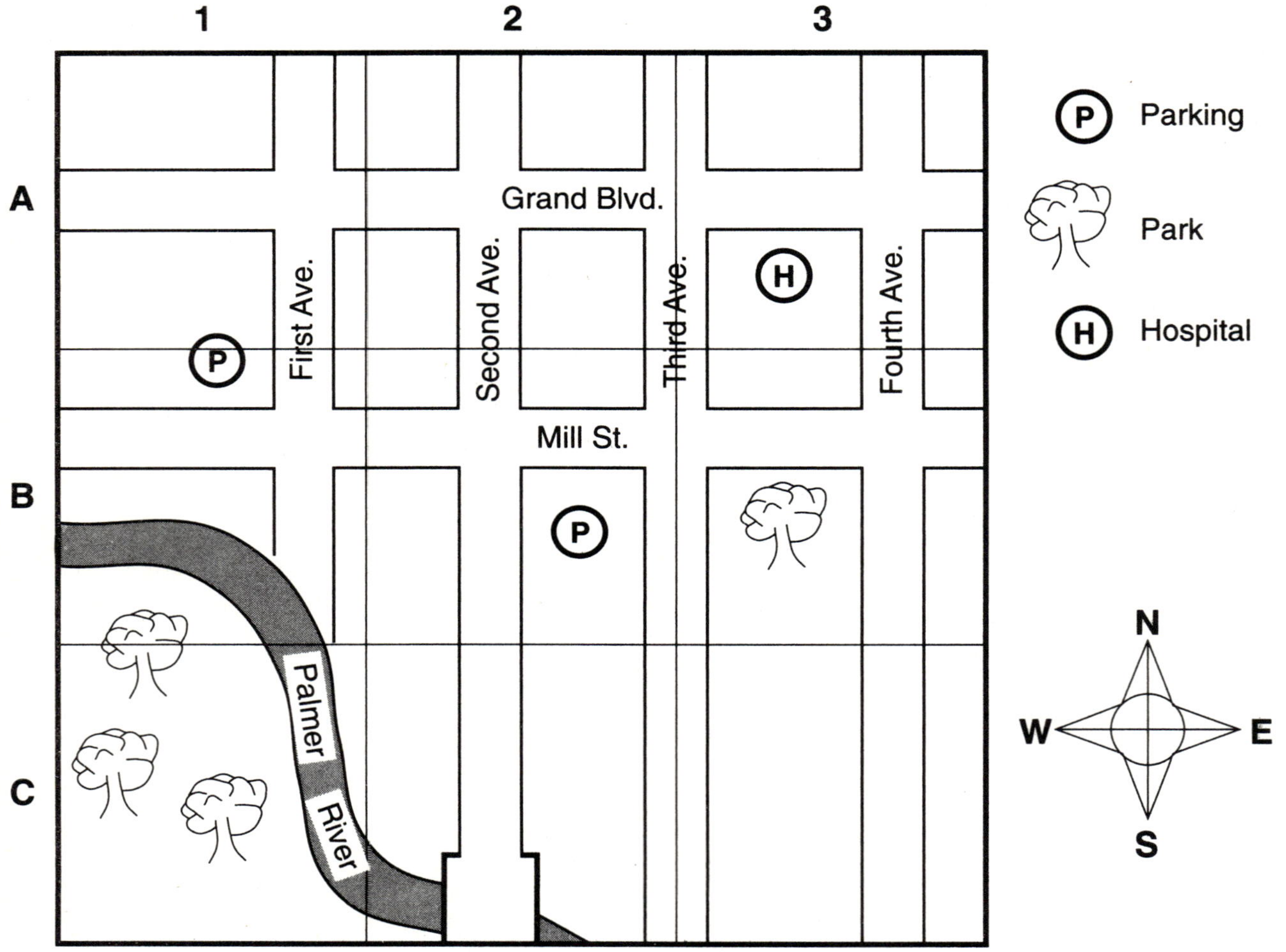

1 Where is the hospital located?

A on Grand between Second and Third
B at First and Mill
C on Grand between Third and Fourth
D on Mill between Second and Third

2 In which section of the map is the park that is east of the river?

F B3
G C1
H C3
J A1

GO

ANSWER ROWS E1 Ⓐ Ⓑ Ⓒ Ⓓ E2 Ⓕ Ⓖ Ⓗ Ⓙ 1 Ⓐ Ⓑ Ⓒ Ⓓ 2 Ⓕ Ⓖ Ⓗ Ⓙ

Use the sample dictionary entries and the Pronunciation Guide below to answer numbers 3-8.

knot [not] *n.* 1. an interlacing of cord or rope 2. a group of people or things 3. a swelling on a body, often caused by an injury 4. the hard piece of wood formed at the joint of a tree trunk and a limb 5. a unit of speed used by sailors equal to 1.15 statute miles per hour *v.* 6. to join two or more ropes or cords together
knowl•edge [nol′ ij] *n.* 1. familiarity with facts, truths, or principles 2. the body of truths accumulated by humans over the course of time
knuck•le [nuk′ əl] *n.* 1. a joint of a finger

Pronunciation Guide:
act, w**ā**y, d**â**re, **ä**rt, s**e**t, **ē**ven, b**i**g, **ī**ce, b**o**x, **ō**ver, h**ô**rse, b**o͝o**k, t**o͞o**l, **u**s, c**ū**te, t**û**rn; **ə** = a in *alone*, e in *mitten*, o in *actor*, u in *circus*

3 The "u" in *knuckle* sounds most like the vowel sound in—

A cute
B turn
C us
D book

4 Which definition best fits the word *knot* as it is used in the sentence below?

A *knot* of men and women gathered in front of the door of the store.

F 2
G 3
H 4
J 5

5 How many syllables are in the word *knowledge*?

A 1
B 2
C 3
D 4

6 In which of these sentences is *knot* used as a verb?

F The knot on Viola's forehead will go down if you put ice on it.
G Were you in the knot of people waiting for the bus?
H The ship was sailing at a speed of about fifteen knots.
J Remember to knot the ends of the rope so it doesn't unravel.

7 Who would most often use the fourth definition of the word *knot*?

A a sailor
B a mail carrier
C a carpenter
D a truck driver

8 Look at the words in the sample dictionary. Which guide words would appear on the dictionary page on which these words are located?

F knack–koala
G know–knurl
H known–Kuwait
J kitchen–knit

GO

ANSWER ROWS 3 Ⓐ Ⓑ Ⓒ Ⓓ 5 Ⓐ Ⓑ Ⓒ Ⓓ 7 Ⓐ Ⓑ Ⓒ Ⓓ
4 Ⓕ Ⓖ Ⓗ Ⓙ 6 Ⓕ Ⓖ Ⓗ Ⓙ 8 Ⓕ Ⓖ Ⓗ Ⓙ

The illustration below shows a set of encyclopedias. Each of the numbered volumes holds information about topics that begin with the letters shown on that volume. Use the picture to do numbers 9-12.

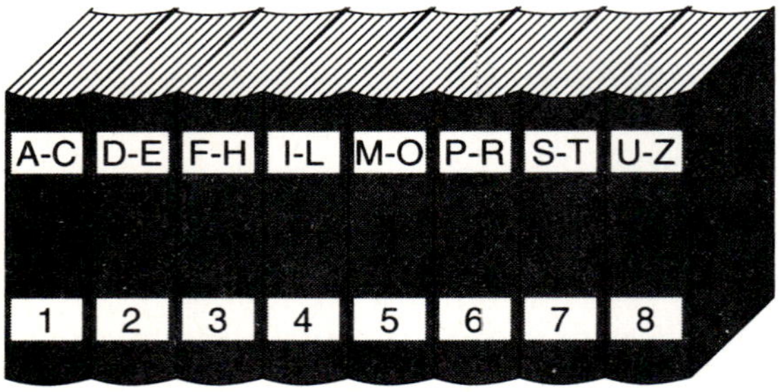

9 Which of these topics would be found in Volume 3?

A a biography of Harriet Tubman
B gardening
C sailing
D how you would find pipes underground

10 In which volume would you find information about pets like cats, dogs, and goldfish?

F Volume 1
G Volume 5
H Volume 2
J Volume 6

11 Which volume might have state maps of Alabama, California, and Delaware?

A Volume 2
B Volume 3
C Volume 5
D Volume 8

12 In which volume would you find the most information about the element nitrogen, which is essential for plant growth?

F Volume 2
G Volume 5
H Volume 6
J Volume 8

Read each question below. Mark the space for the answer you think is correct.

13 Look at these guide words from a dictionary page.

money–movement

Which word could be found on the page?

A moon
B mole
C mower
D moan

14 Look at these guide words from a dictionary page.

stray–strut

Which word could be found on the page?

F strain
G story
H stretch
J stutter

15 Which of these is a main heading that includes the other three words?

A Rings
B Sounds
C Bangs
D Crashes

16 Which of these is a main heading that includes the other three words?

F Milk
G Water
H Liquid
J Juice

STOP

ANSWER ROWS
9 Ⓐ Ⓑ Ⓒ Ⓓ 11 Ⓐ Ⓑ Ⓒ Ⓓ 13 Ⓐ Ⓑ Ⓒ Ⓓ 15 Ⓐ Ⓑ Ⓒ Ⓓ
10 Ⓕ Ⓖ Ⓗ Ⓙ 12 Ⓕ Ⓖ Ⓗ Ⓙ 14 Ⓕ Ⓖ Ⓗ Ⓙ 16 Ⓕ Ⓖ Ⓗ Ⓙ

NUMBER RIGHT ______

Name and Answer Sheet

To the Student:

These tests will give you a chance to put the tips you have learned to work.

A few last reminders…

- Be sure you understand all the directions before you begin each test. You may ask the teacher questions about the directions if you do not understand them.
- Work as quickly as you can during each test.
- When you change an answer, be sure to erase your first mark completely.
- You can guess at an answer or skip difficult items and go back to them later.
- Use the tips you have learned whenever you can.
- It is OK to be a little nervous. You may even do better.

Now that you have completed the lessons in this unit, you are on your way to scoring high!

STUDENT'S NAME

LAST | FIRST | MI

(Each of the 11 LAST columns, the 6 FIRST columns and the MI column has a blank bubble and bubbles A B C D E F G H I J K L M N O P Q R S T U V W X Y Z)

SCHOOL

TEACHER

FEMALE ◯ MALE ◯

BIRTHDATE

MONTH	DAY		YEAR	
JAN ◯	0	0		0
FEB ◯	1	1		1
MAR ◯	2	2		2
APR ◯	3	3		3
MAY ◯		4		4
JUN ◯		5	5	5
JUL ◯		6	6	6
AUG ◯		7	7	7
SEP ◯		8	8	8
OCT ◯		9	9	9
NOV ◯				
DEC ◯				

GRADE

4 5 6

PART 1 LANGUAGE MECHANICS

E1 Ⓐ Ⓑ Ⓒ Ⓓ	**4** Ⓕ Ⓖ Ⓗ Ⓙ	**8** Ⓕ Ⓖ Ⓗ Ⓙ	**12** Ⓕ Ⓖ Ⓗ Ⓙ	**16** Ⓕ Ⓖ Ⓗ Ⓙ	**19** Ⓐ Ⓑ Ⓒ Ⓓ
1 Ⓐ Ⓑ Ⓒ Ⓓ	**5** Ⓐ Ⓑ Ⓒ Ⓓ	**9** Ⓐ Ⓑ Ⓒ Ⓓ	**13** Ⓐ Ⓑ Ⓒ Ⓓ	**17** Ⓐ Ⓑ Ⓒ Ⓓ	**20** Ⓕ Ⓖ Ⓗ Ⓙ
2 Ⓕ Ⓖ Ⓗ Ⓙ	**6** Ⓕ Ⓖ Ⓗ Ⓙ	**10** Ⓕ Ⓖ Ⓗ Ⓙ	**14** Ⓕ Ⓖ Ⓗ Ⓙ	**18** Ⓕ Ⓖ Ⓗ Ⓙ	**21** Ⓐ Ⓑ Ⓒ Ⓓ
3 Ⓐ Ⓑ Ⓒ Ⓓ	**7** Ⓐ Ⓑ Ⓒ Ⓓ	**11** Ⓐ Ⓑ Ⓒ Ⓓ	**15** Ⓐ Ⓑ Ⓒ Ⓓ		

PART 2 LANGUAGE EXPRESSION

E1 Ⓐ Ⓑ Ⓒ Ⓓ	**4** Ⓕ Ⓖ Ⓗ Ⓙ	**8** Ⓕ Ⓖ Ⓗ Ⓙ	**12** Ⓕ Ⓖ Ⓗ Ⓙ	**15** Ⓐ Ⓑ Ⓒ Ⓓ	**18** Ⓕ Ⓖ Ⓗ Ⓙ
1 Ⓐ Ⓑ Ⓒ Ⓓ	**5** Ⓐ Ⓑ Ⓒ Ⓓ	**9** Ⓐ Ⓑ Ⓒ Ⓓ	**13** Ⓐ Ⓑ Ⓒ Ⓓ	**16** Ⓕ Ⓖ Ⓗ Ⓙ	**19** Ⓐ Ⓑ Ⓒ Ⓓ
2 Ⓕ Ⓖ Ⓗ Ⓙ	**6** Ⓕ Ⓖ Ⓗ Ⓙ	**10** Ⓕ Ⓖ Ⓗ Ⓙ	**14** Ⓕ Ⓖ Ⓗ Ⓙ	**17** Ⓐ Ⓑ Ⓒ Ⓓ	**20** Ⓕ Ⓖ Ⓗ Ⓙ
3 Ⓐ Ⓑ Ⓒ Ⓓ	**7** Ⓐ Ⓑ Ⓒ Ⓓ	**11** Ⓐ Ⓑ Ⓒ Ⓓ			

PART 3 SPELLING

E1 Ⓐ Ⓑ Ⓒ Ⓓ	**3** Ⓐ Ⓑ Ⓒ Ⓓ	**7** Ⓐ Ⓑ Ⓒ Ⓓ	**11** Ⓐ Ⓑ Ⓒ Ⓓ Ⓔ	**15** Ⓐ Ⓑ Ⓒ Ⓓ Ⓔ	**19** Ⓐ Ⓑ Ⓒ Ⓓ
E2 Ⓕ Ⓖ Ⓗ Ⓙ	**4** Ⓕ Ⓖ Ⓗ Ⓙ	**8** Ⓕ Ⓖ Ⓗ Ⓙ	**12** Ⓕ Ⓖ Ⓗ Ⓙ Ⓚ	**16** Ⓕ Ⓖ Ⓗ Ⓙ Ⓚ	**20** Ⓕ Ⓖ Ⓗ Ⓙ
1 Ⓐ Ⓑ Ⓒ Ⓓ	**5** Ⓐ Ⓑ Ⓒ Ⓓ	**9** Ⓐ Ⓑ Ⓒ Ⓓ	**13** Ⓐ Ⓑ Ⓒ Ⓓ Ⓔ	**17** Ⓐ Ⓑ Ⓒ Ⓓ Ⓔ	
2 Ⓕ Ⓖ Ⓗ Ⓙ	**6** Ⓕ Ⓖ Ⓗ Ⓙ	**10** Ⓕ Ⓖ Ⓗ Ⓙ	**14** Ⓕ Ⓖ Ⓗ Ⓙ	**18** Ⓕ Ⓖ Ⓗ Ⓙ Ⓚ	

PART 4 STUDY SKILLS

E1 Ⓐ Ⓑ Ⓒ Ⓓ	**3** Ⓐ Ⓑ Ⓒ Ⓓ	**6** Ⓕ Ⓖ Ⓗ Ⓙ	**9** Ⓐ Ⓑ Ⓒ Ⓓ
1 Ⓐ Ⓑ Ⓒ Ⓓ	**4** Ⓕ Ⓖ Ⓗ Ⓙ	**7** Ⓐ Ⓑ Ⓒ Ⓓ	**10** Ⓕ Ⓖ Ⓗ Ⓙ
2 Ⓕ Ⓖ Ⓗ Ⓙ	**5** Ⓐ Ⓑ Ⓒ Ⓓ	**8** Ⓕ Ⓖ Ⓗ Ⓙ	

Part 1 Language Mechanics

Example **Directions:** Fill in the space for the choice that has a punctuation error. If there is no mistake, fill in the fourth answer space.

E1

The elevator in our building is broken

A . **B** ! **C** ? **D** None

1 Which way is the hotel?" asked Mr. Harrison.

A ? **B** , **C** " **D** None

2 Hurry, the storm will start any minute

F ? **G** . **H** ! **J** None

3 Does your dog like to chase a ball?

A . **B** , **C** ! **D** None

4 No we can't go to the lake this Sunday.

F , **G** ? **H** : **J** None

For numbers 5-7, read each answer. Fill in the space for the choice that has a punctuation error. If there is no mistake, fill in the fourth answer space.

5 **A** In Denver Colorado
B you can get a good look
C at the Rocky Mountains.
D *(No mistakes)*

6 **F** How did you know
G our phone number. We
H moved last month.
J *(No mistakes)*

7 **A** Flo went to the auto
B parts store with her father.
C They bought oil and a filter.
D *(No mistakes)*

For numbers 8 and 9, read each sentence with a blank. Choose the word or words that fit best in the blank and show the correct punctuation.

8 We helped ________ family move into their new apartment.

F Dominics
G Dominics'
H Dominic's
J Dominics's

9 Rosa came with ________ her brother stayed home.

A us but
B us, but,
C us but,
D us, but

GO

For numbers 10-13, read each group of sentences. Find the one that is written correctly and shows the correct capitalization and punctuation.

10 **F** Nelson shouldnt eat so much if he is going to swim this afternoon.

G A work crew is repairing the road damage on waterford avenue.

H how will you know when the turkey is finished?

J The book *Old Yeller* wasn't in the library the last time I looked.

11 **A** The homework you handed in yesterday is very good, Meg.

B Raj did you remember your permission slip for the class trip?

C if you hurry Allie you can catch the bus before it leaves.

D Our school held a computer fair for the other school's in the district.

12 **F** Our town has a parade, and a picnic on the third Saturday in July.

G Fran, Maida, and Matthew will visit us sometime in June.

H In april we had a week of nothing but wind rain and clouds.

J We had our smallest electricity, and telephone, bills in january.

13 **A** What is your favorite food, mine is pizza with pepperoni and extra cheese.

B The apples are in the refrigerator, But the bananas are in a bowl on the table.

C The spaghetti is delicious. May I have some more?

D It's so nice outside? We should eat our supper on the deck.

For numbers 14-16, read the sentence with a blank. Mark the space beside the answer choice that fits best in the blank and has correct capitalization and punctuation.

14 Our school is on ________ near the bank.

F Harper, St.
G harper st.
H Harper St,
J Harper St.

15 ________ likes to sit under my desk when I do my homework.

A nick my dog
B Nick my dog,
C Nick, my dog,
D Nick. My dog

16 The ________ is visited by more than three million people a year.

F Statue of Liberty
G Statue of Liberty,
H statue of Liberty
J statue of liberty

Choose the correct answer for number 17.

17 Which is the correct way to begin a friendly letter?

A Dear Angela.
B Dear Angela,
C Dear Angela
D Dear Angela;

Holly is writing an article for her local newspaper about an historic house in her neighborhood. Read the article and use it to do numbers 18-21.

(1) The Bunnell House was started by Zebulon Bunnell in the spring of 1795. **(2)** He began by hiring some workers to clear the trees' from a few acres of land and cut them into rough lumber. **(3)** While the workers were cutting the trees Zebulon and his brother gathered stones to use for the foundation of the house. **(4)** It took them a few months to build the house. **(5)** The house was not large, but it was comfortable. **(6)** A spring was right beside the house, so there was plenty of fresh water.

(7) Mr. Bunnell was a dairy farmer he worked very hard, and in a few years had enough money to add another room to his small house. **(8)** He married Clare Bonham and they had three children. **(9)** They decided to add another room to the house.

18 In sentence 2, trees' is best written —

- **F** tree's
- **G** trees's
- **H** trees
- **J** As it is

19 In sentence 3, trees Zebulon is best written —

- **A** trees, Zebulon
- **B** trees zebulon
- **C** trees. Zebulon
- **D** As it is

20 In sentence 5, large, but is best written —

- **F** large but
- **G** large but,
- **H** large. But
- **J** As it is

21 In sentence 7, farmer he worked is best written —

- **A** farmer, he worked
- **B** farmer. He worked
- **C** Farmer he worked
- **D** As it is

STOP

Part 2 Language Expression

Example **Directions:** Find the underlined part that is the simple subject of the sentence.

E1

Find the underlined part that is the simple subject of the sentence.

The happy children chased after the dog with a stick.

A: The — B: children — C: chased — D: dog

For number 1, choose the word or phrase that best completes the sentence.

1 Our class ________ a bake sale to raise money for a computer.

- **A** hold
- **B** holding
- **C** is being held
- **D** will hold

For number 2, choose the answer that is a complete and correctly written sentence.

2 **F** The mayor invited us class to a meeting of the town council.

- **G** My sisters made theirselves sandwiches for lunch.
- **H** Paul and I walked to the store even though it was raining.
- **J** Me and Olivia would rather stay home than go for a ride.

For numbers 3-5, read each answer choice. Fill in the space for the choice that has a usage error. If there is no mistake, fill in the fourth answer space.

3 **A** My cousins liketa

- **B** come to our house because
- **C** we have a basketball court.
- **D** *(No mistakes)*

4 **F** Mr. Nolan hurt his knee

- **G** while he was working in the garden.
- **H** It will be better soon.
- **J** *(No mistakes)*

5 **A** The owner of the old car

- **B** didn't want no one
- **C** to touch it without permission.
- **D** *(No mistakes)*

For number 6, find the underlined part that is the simple subject of the sentence.

6 Your running shoes are in the living room.

F: Your — G: running — H: shoes — J: living

For number 7, find the underlined part that is the simple predicate (verb) of the sentence.

7 Trees grow in some very unusual places.

A: Trees — B: grow — C: some — D: places

GO

For numbers 8-10, choose the answer that best combines the underlined sentences.

8 The car is in the parking lot.

The car has a flat tire.

F The car is in the parking lot, and the car has a flat tire.
G In the parking lot is the car that has a flat tire.
H The car in the parking lot has a flat tire.
J With a flat tire, the car is in the parking lot.

9 Ms. Martinez is our mail carrier.

Ms. Martinez lives next door to us.

A Ms. Martinez, who is our mail carrier, who lives next door to us.
B Ms. Martinez, living next door to us, is also our mail carrier.
C Ms. Martinez, who is our mail carrier, and who lives next door to us.
D Ms. Martinez, our mail carrier, lives next door to us.

10 The house on the hill is large.

The house is white.

The house has a green roof.

F With a green roof, the large white house is on the hill.
G The large house is on the hill, and it is white and it has a green roof.
H The large house on the hill is white with a green roof.
J On the large hill is a white house with a green roof.

For numbers 11 and 12, choose the best way of expressing the idea.

11 **A** The electronic encyclopedia that came with our new computer.
B Our new computer came with an electronic encyclopedia.
C Our new computer, which came with an electronic encyclopedia.
D Coming with an electronic encyclopedia is our new computer.

12 **F** After our Oregon trip, our friends we showed many photographs.
G After our trip to Oregon, we had many photographs to show our friends.
H We had many photographs after our trip to Oregon to show our friends.
J Our friends, after our trip to Oregon, were shown many photographs.

Read the paragraph below. Find the best topic sentence for the paragraph.

13 ________________ . Owned by Beverly and Jeff Timmons, the Craft Emporium has supplies for all kinds of creative activities. The store is open every day from 10:00 AM to 6:00 PM and offers discounts to frequent shoppers.

A A new craft store has opened in the Sunset Shopping Center.

B The Sunset Shopping Center is at the corner of Ninth and Harvest.

C Many people enjoy different kinds of crafts.

D Beverly and Jeff Timmons turned their hobby into a business.

Find the answer choice that best develops the topic sentence.

14 Many individuals and communities in the West are creating gardens that consume as little water as possible.

F Lawns require a great deal of water, especially in dry years. You also must mow them often and fertilize them at least once a year.

G Plants like cactus are included in a xeriscape garden. There are hundreds of different cactus types available today.

H In much of the West it is hot and dry. Plants that do well in the East can't survive in this climate unless they are watered often.

J Called xeriscaping, this type of gardening makes use of native plants that thrive in dry conditions. A well-designed xeriscape garden is easy to take care of and looks attractive.

Read the paragraph below. Find the sentence that does not belong in the paragraph.

15 1. Dorothea Lange was a world-class photographer. 2. Her most famous photographs were of farm people moving west during the Great Depression. 3. The Great Depression began in 1929 with a stock market crash. 4. Lange's photography captured both the fears and hopes of these migrant workers.

A Sentence 1

B Sentence 2

C Sentence 3

D Sentence 4

Read the paragraph below. Find the sentence that best fits the blank in the paragraph.

16 Humans have trained many unusual animals to work for them. ________________. Water buffalo are hitched to plows and work in rice paddies in parts of Asia. Elephants are trained in India to do heavy work such as moving logs.

F An unusual pet is the iguana, a kind of lizard.

G Falcons have been used to hunt for over a thousand years.

H Machines are also used to do certain jobs.

J Horses were introduced to America by Spanish explorers.

GO

Below is more of Holly's article about an old house in her neighborhood. Read the story and use it to do numbers 17-20.

> **(1)** By 1830, Zebulon Pike was one of the most successful farmers in the area. **(2)** He added several more rooms to his home. **(3)** Pike also had the outside painted white. **(4)** Clare furnished the inside of the house with things she ordered from Boston and Philadelphia. **(5)** Newspaper reports from the time the house as "the most beautiful home in the county."
>
> **(6)** Zebulon Pike was killed in a farming accident in 1853. **(7)** His wife sold the house and the farm to Samuel Wright in 1854. **(8)** The first thing he did was add three more rooms to the house, including an elegant living room. **(9)** With a few minor changes, the house that Samuel Wright living in from 1854 until his death in 1888 is the same house that stands on Watts Street today.

17 How would sentences 2 and 3 best be combined without changing their meaning?

- **A** He added several more rooms to his home, which was white.
- **B** Having the outside painted white, he added several more rooms.
- **C** He added several more rooms to his home and had the outside painted white.
- **D** Because he added more rooms to his home, he had the outside painted white.

18 Which group of words is not a complete thought?

- **F** 1
- **G** 5
- **H** 6
- **J** 8

19 How is sentence 7 best written?

- **A** His wife, in 1854, sold the house to Samuel Wright, and the farm.
- **B** In 1854, his wife, who sold the house and farm to Samuel Wright.
- **C** Selling the house and farm to Samuel Wright in 1854.
- **D** As it is

20 In sentence 9, living in is best written —

- **F** lived in
- **G** live in
- **H** were living in
- **J** As it is

STOP

Part 3 Spelling

Examples

Directions: For E1, find the word that is spelled correctly and fits best in the blank. For E2, choose the phrase in which the underlined word is not spelled correctly.

E1

What did the company ________ you?

A ofer
B ofir
C offir
D offer

E2

F relacksing vacation

G on the stage

H unfair rules

J enjoyed a movie

For numbers 1-6, find the word that is spelled correctly and fits best in the blank.

1 We had ________ for dinner.

A shremp
B schrimp
C shreimp
D shrimp

2 An ________ rock fell into the road.

F enormous
G inormous
H enormus
J enormis

3 Connie will ________ for her driver's license.

A aply
B applie
C apply
D appliy

4 The cat ________ the birds in the tree.

F watcht
G wached
H watched
J watchted

5 The fisherman used a ________ lure.

A shinie
B shiny
C shiney
D shynie

6 Who is the store ________ ?

F manager
G maneger
H manger
J mananger

For numbers 7-10, read the phrases. Choose the phrase in which the underlined word is not spelled correctly.

7 **A** follow a trail

B loud sneeze

C crowd of people

D escaped to freedim

8 **F** history book

G feel concirn

H good suggestion

J grateful for help

9 **A** diffrent locations

B huge parade

C always happy

D sharp knife

10 **F** rain is possible

G remote control

H paynted a door

J mysterious sound

For numbers 11-13, read each answer. Fill in the space for the choice that has a spelling error. If there is no mistake, fill in the last answer space.

11
- **A** nicely
- **B** straight
- **C** damaged
- **D** discribe
- **E** *(No mistakes)*

12
- **F** promise
- **G** imaginery
- **H** avenue
- **J** major
- **K** *(No mistakes)*

13
- **A** restaurant
- **B** children
- **C** expected
- **D** liberty
- **E** *(No mistakes)*

For numbers 14-16, read each phrase. One of the underlined words is not spelled correctly for the way it is used in the phrase. Fill in the space for the word that is not spelled correctly.

14
- **F** crisp bacon
- **G** high sealing
- **H** observe an accident
- **J** hollow log

15
- **A** brake an egg
- **B** valuable painting
- **C** delicious fruit
- **D** great athlete

16
- **F** exact change
- **G** difficult puzzle
- **H** nearly finished
- **J** would from a tree

For numbers 17-20, find the underlined part that is misspelled. If all words are spelled correctly, mark the space under No mistake.

17 A livly group of visitors entered the museum. No mistake.
A (livly) **B** (visitors) **C** (museum) **D** (No mistake)

18 In which period do you have science? No mistake.
F (which) **G** (period) **H** (science) **J** (No mistake)

19 The bowls are in the cabinit in the kitchen. No mistake.
A (bowls) **B** (cabinit) **C** (kitchen) **D** (No mistake)

20 Somtimes people do things they are sorry for. No mistake.
F (Somtimes) **G** (people) **H** (sorry) **J** (No mistake)

Example

Directions: Study the outline, then choose the answer you think is correct.

OUTLINE
Water Sports
1. Swimming
2. Fishing
3. Boating
4. ________
5. Scuba Diving

E1

Which of these would fit best in Line 4 of the outline on the left?

A Surfing
B Beach Formation
C Ocean Tides
D Jogging

Study the map below. Use it to do numbers 1 and 2.

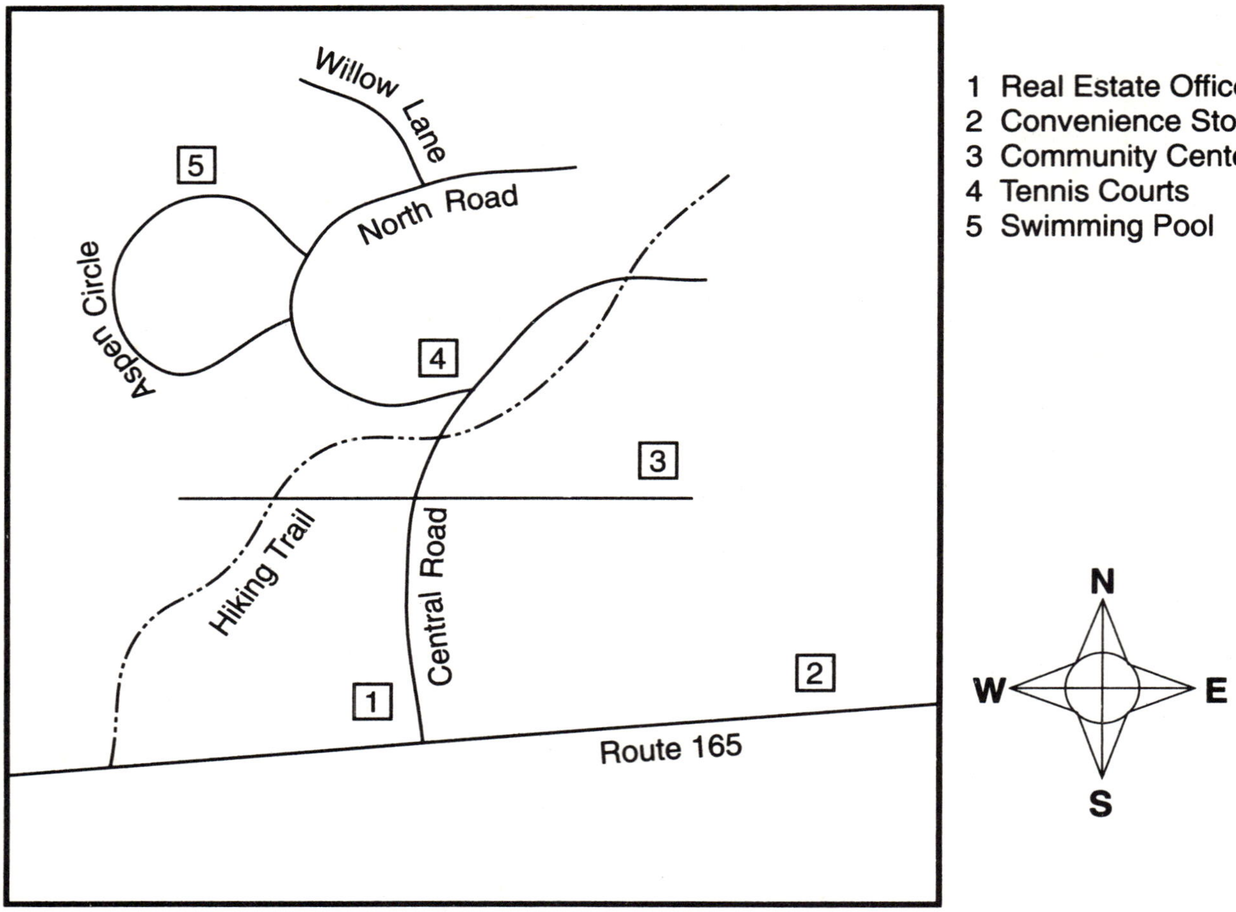

1 Real Estate Office
2 Convenience Store
3 Community Center
4 Tennis Courts
5 Swimming Pool

1 The hiking trail begins at Route 165. In what general direction does the hiking trail go?

A southeast
B southwest
C northwest
D northeast

2 Where are the tennis courts located?

F on Aspen Circle
G at the corner of North and Central Roads
H at the corner of Central Road and Route 165
J on Route 165

GO

Use this card from a library card catalog to do numbers 3-6.

201.64

Ha **Harris, Patricia Walker**
Business Success at Home / Patricia W. Harris; photographs and charts by George Rosen. Foreword by Richard Babcock.
San Francisco: Bay Publishing Company, 1993.
320 pages; photos and charts; 23 cm
(The Home Office series, volume 4)

1. Business 2. Success and business 3. Home office I. Title

3 What is the title of this book?

A *Success and Business*
B *Home Office*
C *Business Success at Home*
D *Business*

4 What did Richard Babcock have to do with this book?

F He wrote the foreword.
G He is the author.
H He published the book.
J He took the photographs.

5 In which section of the card catalog would this card be found?

A Title
B Subject
C Publisher
D Author

6 How many pages are in this book?

F 201
G 23
H 320
J 1993

Read each question below. Mark the space for the answer you think is correct.

7 Look at these guide words from a dictionary page.

stand–state

Which word could be found on the page?

A stance
B stay
C standard
D status

8 Look at these guide words from a dictionary page.

crisp–cut

Which word could be found on the page?

F crop
G crib
H cute
J crane

9 Which of these is a main heading that includes the other three words?

A Cars
B Trucks
C Buses
D Vehicles

10 Which of these might be found in a book chapter entitled "Unusual Hobbies?"

F collecting stamps
G collecting coins
H collecting light bulbs
J collecting old books

STOP

Table of Contents

Math

Lesson 1 Numeration

Example

Directions: Read and work each problem. Find the correct answer. Mark the space for your choice.

A Which two numbers are both factors of 45?

- **A** 4, 5
- **B** 4, 15
- **C** 5, 9
- **D** 5, 40

B Which of these is between 1.05 and 1.5 in value?

- **F** 0.95
- **G** 1.55
- **H** 1.72
- **J** 1.27

Tips

Read each question carefully. Look for key words and numbers that will help you find the answers.

Be sure the answer circle you fill in is the same letter as the answer you think is correct.

Practice

1 100 =

- **A** 1^{10}
- **B** 2^{5}
- **C** 5^{3}
- **D** 10^{2}

2 Which of these will have a remainder when it is divided by 9?

- **F** 27
- **G** 29
- **H** 36
- **J** 45

3 Your friend is twelfth in line for a roller coaster ride. Exactly how many people are ahead of your friend?

- **A** 10
- **B** 11
- **C** 14
- **D** 17

4 Which point on this number line shows 473?

- **F** A
- **G** B
- **H** C
- **J** D

5 What number is expressed by

(7 x 1000) + (2 x 100) + (1 x 10) + (1 x 1)

- **A** 7210
- **B** 7211
- **C** 70,101
- **D** 7200

GO

ANSWER ROWS A Ⓐ Ⓑ Ⓒ Ⓓ 1 Ⓐ Ⓑ Ⓒ Ⓓ 3 Ⓐ Ⓑ Ⓒ Ⓓ 5 Ⓐ Ⓑ Ⓒ Ⓓ
B Ⓕ Ⓖ Ⓗ Ⓙ 2 Ⓕ Ⓖ Ⓗ Ⓙ 4 Ⓕ Ⓖ Ⓗ Ⓙ

6 What is the meaning of 780?

F 7 tens and 8 ones

G 8 tens and 7 ones

H 7 hundreds and 8 ones

J 7 hundreds and 8 tens

7 How many of these numbers are common multiples of 5 and 7?

25	35	60	70	77	105

A 2

B 3

C 4

D 5

8 Which of these numbers cannot be evenly divided into 16?

F 1

G 3

H 4

J 8

9 Which of these is the expanded numeral for 8927?

A 89 + 27

B 800 + 900 + 200 + 7

C 9000 + 800 + 20 + 7

D 8000 + 900 + 20 + 7

10 What is the smallest number that can be divided evenly by 7 and 16?

F 34

G 56

H 112

J 224

11 Which of these is not another way to write the number 2009?

A 2000 + 9

B 2 thousands, 9 ones

C two thousand nine

D

thousands	hundreds	tens	ones
2	0	9	0

12 A department store worker was putting shirts on shelves. There were 40 shirts and 7 shelves. The worker wanted to put the same number of shirts on each shelf and discovered there were some extras. How many shirts did not fit on the 7 shelves?

F 5

G 4

H 3

J 2

13 Which of these is the greatest common factor of 18 and 27?

A 3

B 7

C 9

D 18

14 $\sqrt{25}$ =

F 5

G 6

H 10

J 12

STOP

ANSWER ROWS 6 Ⓕ Ⓖ Ⓗ Ⓙ 8 Ⓕ Ⓖ Ⓗ Ⓙ 10 Ⓕ Ⓖ Ⓗ Ⓙ 12 Ⓕ Ⓖ Ⓗ Ⓙ 14 Ⓕ Ⓖ Ⓗ Ⓙ

7 Ⓐ Ⓑ Ⓒ Ⓓ 9 Ⓐ Ⓑ Ⓒ Ⓓ 11 Ⓐ Ⓑ Ⓒ Ⓓ 13 Ⓐ Ⓑ Ⓒ Ⓓ

Example

Directions: Read and work each problem. Find the correct answer. Mark the space for your choice.

A Which of these has a 2 in the tens place?

A 2132
B 32
C 211
D 121

B Which of these is an odd number?

F 43
G 22
H 38
J 56

Tips

Key words, numbers, pictures, and figures will help you find the answers.

Eliminate answer choices you know are wrong.

Practice

1 What is another name for the Roman numeral VII?

A 2
B 7
C 12
D 522

2 What rule can you use to find the number that is missing from the pattern below?

3, 6, 10, 20, ___, 48

F add 4 to 20
G multiply 20 by 2
H add 10 to 20
J multiply 6 by 3

3 Which statement about place value is true?

A 10 thousands are equal to 1000
B 10 thousands are equal to 100,000
C 10 hundreds are equal to 1000
D 10 hundreds are equal to 10,000

4 597,346 =

F five million, ninety-seven thousand, three hundred forty-six

G five hundred ninety-seven million, three hundred forty-six

H five hundred ninety-seven, three hundred forty-six

J five hundred ninety-seven thousand, three hundred forty-six

5 Which of these statements is true about the numbers in the box?

2, 5, 13, 29, 61

A They are all even numbers.
B They are all odd numbers.
C They are all prime numbers.
D They are all odd and are also prime numbers.

GO

ANSWER ROWS

A Ⓐ Ⓑ Ⓒ Ⓓ	1 Ⓐ Ⓑ Ⓒ Ⓓ	3 Ⓐ Ⓑ Ⓒ Ⓓ	5 Ⓐ Ⓑ Ⓒ Ⓓ	
B Ⓕ Ⓖ Ⓗ Ⓙ	2 Ⓕ Ⓖ Ⓗ Ⓙ	4 Ⓕ Ⓖ Ⓗ Ⓙ		

6 How much would the value of 19,527 be decreased by replacing the 5 with a 2?

F 200
G 300
H 2000
J 3000

7 Which of these numbers is both even and a multiple of 7?

A 22
B 27
C 35
D 42

8 Which of these is 7,207,354?

F seven million, two hundred thousand, three hundred fifty-four

G seven hundred twenty-seven thousand, three hundred fifty-four

H seven million, two hundred seven thousand, three hundred fifty-four

J seven million, twenty-seven thousand, three hundred fifty-four

9 Suppose you have the digits 3, 7, and 8. Without repeating a digit, how many three-digit numbers can you make with 7 as the hundreds digit?

A 2
B 3
C 6
D 7

10 These squares show groups of numbers that are related by the same rule. What number is missing from the second square?

135	45
15	5

54	18
?	2

108	36
12	4

F 12
G 8
H 6
J 4

11 In which of these numerals does 9 have the greatest value?

A 1932
B 395
C 3829
D 98

12 What does the 3 in 239,048 mean?

F 3
G 3000
H 300,000
J 30,000

13 Which is the numeral for six million, three hundred seventy-nine thousand, five hundred forty-one?

A 637,541
B 6,379,541
C 6,397,541
D 637,941

STOP

Lesson 3 Properties

Example

Directions: Read and work each problem. Find the correct answer. Mark the space for your choice.

A What is another name for 7 + (2 x 5)?

A (7 + 2) x 5

B 7 + (5 x 2)

C (5 x 2) – 7

D (7 – 5) x 2

B What is 455,398 rounded to the nearest thousand?

F 455,390

G 455,400

H 450,000

J 455,000

Tips

Sometimes you won't have to compute to find the answer to a problem. For this type of problem, it's especially important to look for key words and numbers that will help you find the answer.

Look at all the answer choices before selecting the one you think is correct.

Practice

1 The sum of 589 and 921 is closest to —

A 1600

B 1500

C 1400

D 1300

2 Which number sentence below is incorrect?

F 3 + 0 = 3

G 3 – 0 = 3

H 0 x 3 = 0

J 0 ÷ 3 = 3

3 Another name for 30 x 1000 is —

A 300 x 100

B 30,000 x 100

C 3 x 1000

D 3000 x 1000

4 What number makes all the number sentences below true?

6 x □ = 12
□ x 10 = 20
9 x □ = 18

F 3

G 4

H 2

J 5

5 A factory has 314 workers. The owner gave each worker a bonus of $1950. Which number sentence shows how to find the total amount of bonus money the owner paid?

A $1950 + 314 = □

B $1950 x 314 = □

C $1950 – 314 = □

D $1950 ÷ 314 = □

GO

ANSWER ROWS **A** Ⓐ Ⓑ Ⓒ Ⓓ **1** Ⓐ Ⓑ Ⓒ Ⓓ **3** Ⓐ Ⓑ Ⓒ Ⓓ **5** Ⓐ Ⓑ Ⓒ Ⓓ
B Ⓕ Ⓖ Ⓗ Ⓙ **2** Ⓕ Ⓖ Ⓗ Ⓙ **4** Ⓕ Ⓖ Ⓗ Ⓙ

6 The amounts below show how much a student earned each week during July.

$28.50 $37.20 $32.80 $44.10

What is the best estimate to the nearest ten dollars of the total amount the student earned in July?

F $150

G $140

H $110

J $90

7 What numbers should go in the square and circle to make this division problem true?

499 ÷ 8 = □2 R○

A □ = 6, ○ = 2

B □ = 8, ○ = 2

C □ = 2, ○ = 6

D □ = 6, ○ = 3

8 What is 385,001 rounded to the nearest hundred thousand?

F 100,000

G 350,000

H 390,000

J 400,000

9 Which of the following number facts does not belong to the same family or group as the number sentence in the box?

4 x 9 = 36

A 36 ÷ 4 = 9

B 36 ÷ 6 = 6

C 36 ÷ 9 = 4

D 9 x 4 = 36

10 Which of these is the best estimate of 89 x 105?

F 80 x 100

G 90 x 100

H 90 x 110

J 80 x 110

11 What symbol should replace the box in the number sentence below?

16 □ 9 = 21 ÷ 3

A −

B +

C x

D ÷

12 What should replace the circle below to make the number sentence true?

14 + 6 ○ 40 ÷ 10

F =

G <

H >

J +

13 Which statement is true about the number sentence in the box?

6896 ÷ 1000 = □

A □ is less than 5.

B □ is between 5 and 6.

C □ is equal to 6.

D □ is between 6 and 7.

STOP

ANSWER ROWS
6 Ⓕ Ⓖ Ⓗ Ⓙ 8 Ⓕ Ⓖ Ⓗ Ⓙ 10 Ⓕ Ⓖ Ⓗ Ⓙ 12 Ⓕ Ⓖ Ⓗ Ⓙ
7 Ⓐ Ⓑ Ⓒ Ⓓ 9 Ⓐ Ⓑ Ⓒ Ⓓ 11 Ⓐ Ⓑ Ⓒ Ⓓ 13 Ⓐ Ⓑ Ⓒ Ⓓ

Example

Directions: Read and work each problem. Find the correct answer. Mark the space for your choice.

A Which fraction is shown by the X on this number line?

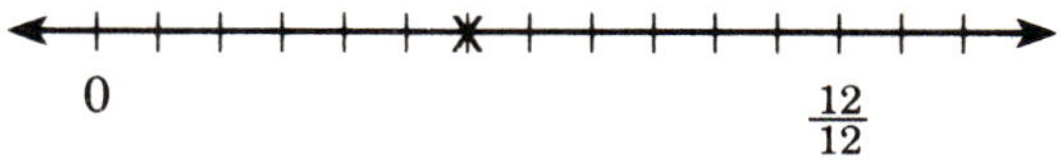

A $\frac{1}{7}$

B $\frac{2}{5}$

C $\frac{7}{12}$

D $\frac{1}{2}$

Tips

If you work on scratch paper, be sure you transfer numbers correctly.

Pay close attention to the numbers in the problem and in the answer choices. If you misread even one number, you will probably choose the wrong answer.

Practice

1 Which figure below is $\frac{5}{12}$ shaded?

A 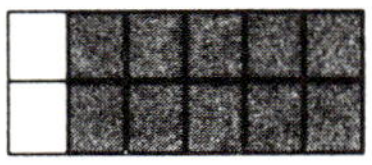

B 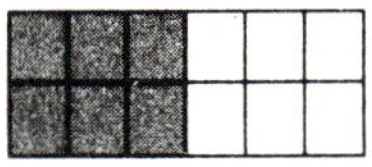

C 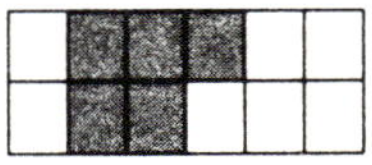

D 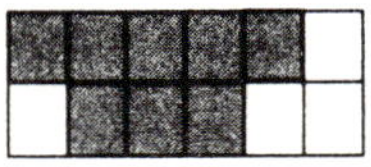

2 Which of these is another way to write $\frac{6}{9}$?

F $\frac{2}{3}$

G $\frac{9}{6}$

H $\frac{12}{15}$

J $\frac{16}{19}$

3 The length of $\overline{AB}$ is what fraction of the length of $\overline{CD}$?

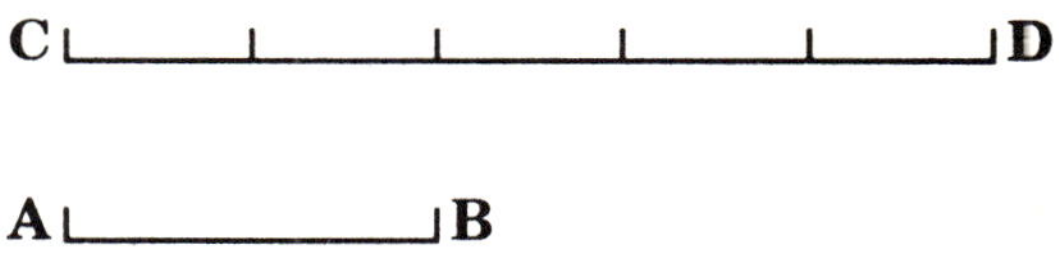

A $\frac{2}{3}$

B $\frac{2}{5}$

C $\frac{1}{5}$

D $\frac{1}{2}$

4 Which group of decimals is ordered from least to greatest?

F 5.892, 5.721, 5.439, 5.192

G 5.629, 5.175, 5.628, 5.394

H 5.173, 5.742, 5.206, 5.819

J 5.229, 5.711, 5.806, 5.843

GO

5 Which decimal tells how much of this shape is shaded?

A 0.35

B 0.73

C 0.57

D 0.53

6 $\frac{1}{\square} = \frac{18}{36}$

$\square =$

F 2

G 3

H 4

J 6

7 Which of these has a value less than $\frac{1}{4}$?

A $\frac{2}{3}$

B $\frac{3}{5}$

C $\frac{1}{3}$

D $\frac{1}{5}$

8 Which of these is between 0.12 and 0.21 in value?

F 0.09

G 0.18

H 0.52

J 0.74

9 How should you write forty-one hundredths as a decimal?

A 41.00

B 4.1

C 0.41

D 0.04

10 Which number tells how much of this group of shapes is shaded?

F $\frac{1}{5}$

G $2\frac{8}{9}$

H $2\frac{4}{5}$

J $1\frac{1}{9}$

11 Which letter marks $4\frac{1}{4}$ on this number line?

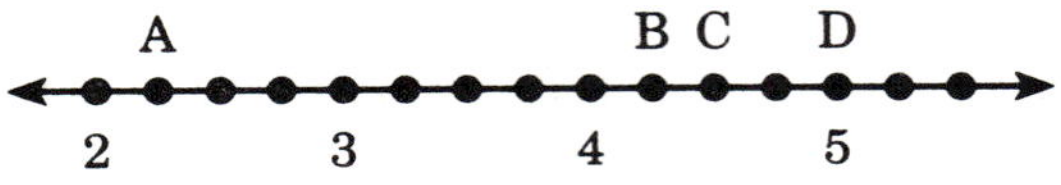

A A

B B

C C

D D

12 What is the least common denominator of $\frac{1}{3}$, $\frac{1}{5}$, and $\frac{1}{6}$?

F 10

G 15

H 30

J 60

STOP

Lesson 5 Test Yourself

Examples

Directions: Read and work each problem. Find the correct answer. Mark the space for your choice.

E1

$\frac{159}{1000} =$

A 1.59

B 0.159

C 0.1509

D 0.1059

E2

What is the value of y in the number sentence $40 \div y = 8$?

F 5

G 6

H 3

J 32

1 Which of these is between 558,390 and 585,093?

A 593,085

B 553,855

C 590,390

D 580,935

2 Which of these is the same as the number in the place-value chart?

1000s	100s	10s	1s
8	3	9	1

F 8931

G eight thousand three hundred ninety-one

H 8 thousands 391 hundreds

J 8000 + 3100 + 910 + 1

3 What decimal goes in the box on the number line below?

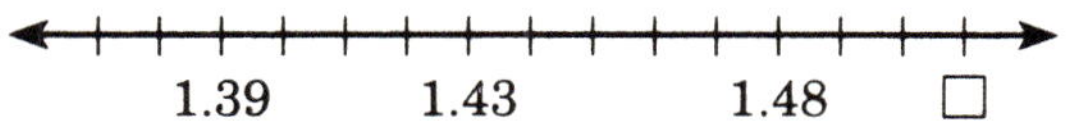

A 1.51

B 1.49

C 1.52

D 1.46

4 What is the value of 3 in 24.53?

F 3 hundredths

G 3 thousandths

H 3 tens

J 3 tenths

5 What are all the factors of the product of 6 x 3?

A 2, 4, and 8

B 1, 3, 5, 6, and 15

C 1, 2, 3, 6, 9, and 18

D 1, 2, 3, 4, 6, 8, 9, and 18

6 If the pattern formed by the shaded blocks was continued, how many would be shaded in the last figure?

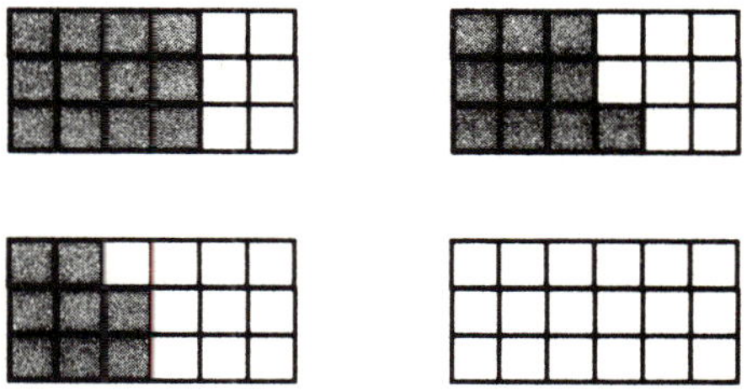

F 9

G 7

H 6

J 0

GO

ANSWER ROWS
E1 Ⓐ Ⓑ Ⓒ Ⓓ 1 Ⓐ Ⓑ Ⓒ Ⓓ 3 Ⓐ Ⓑ Ⓒ Ⓓ 5 Ⓐ Ⓑ Ⓒ Ⓓ
E2 Ⓕ Ⓖ Ⓗ Ⓙ 2 Ⓕ Ⓖ Ⓗ Ⓙ 4 Ⓕ Ⓖ Ⓗ Ⓙ 6 Ⓕ Ⓖ Ⓗ Ⓙ

7 Suppose you wanted to double the number 8 and then add 10 to it. Which number sentence would you use?

A (8 x 2) + 10 = ☐

B 8 + 2 + 10 = ☐

C 8 x 2 x 10 = ☐

D (2 x 10) + 8 = ☐

8 Which of these numbers is less than the Roman numeral IX?

F 21

G 10

H 8

J 9

9 Which of these rules is correct?

A Half of any even number is odd.

B Half of any even number is even.

C All odd numbers can be divided by 3.

D All even numbers can be divided by 2.

10 Which number is closest in value to the shaded portion of this figure?

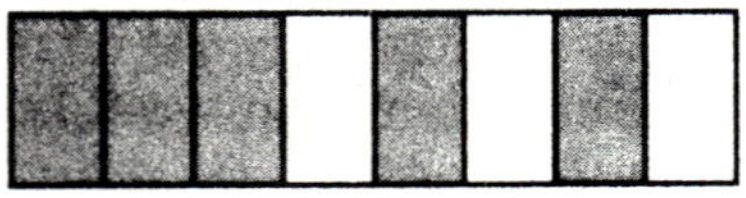

F 0.5

G 0.65

H 0.75

J 0.8

11 Which is another name for 21 x 100?

A 211 x 10

B 210 x 10

C 21 x 1000

D 210 x 100

12 In which numeral is there a 5 in both the tens and the ten thousands place?

F 1,505,925

G 5,501,658

H 7,356,259

J 2,459,519

13 What number is one thousand less than 8292?

A 7292

B 9292

C 8192

D 8291

14 Which of these is another name for $\frac{2}{9}$?

F $\frac{4}{19}$

G $\frac{12}{54}$

H $\frac{8}{32}$

J $\frac{7}{14}$

15 What number makes these number sentences true?

$\square + 21 = 30$

$63 \div 7 = \square$

A 19

B 8

C 11

D 9

16 Which of these is a prime number?

F 12

G 15

H 17

J 21

STOP

ANSWER ROWS
7 Ⓐ Ⓑ Ⓒ Ⓓ 10 Ⓕ Ⓖ Ⓗ Ⓙ 13 Ⓐ Ⓑ Ⓒ Ⓓ 15 Ⓐ Ⓑ Ⓒ Ⓓ
8 Ⓕ Ⓖ Ⓗ Ⓙ 11 Ⓐ Ⓑ Ⓒ Ⓓ 14 Ⓕ Ⓖ Ⓗ Ⓙ 16 Ⓕ Ⓖ Ⓗ Ⓙ
9 Ⓐ Ⓑ Ⓒ Ⓓ 12 Ⓕ Ⓖ Ⓗ Ⓙ

NUMBER RIGHT______

Lesson 6 Addition

Example

Directions: Mark the space for the correct answer to each addition problem. Choose "None of these" if the right answer is not given.

A

$$\begin{array}{r} 17 \\ +\ 13 \\ \hline \end{array}$$

A 3
B 21
C 4
D 30
E None of these

B

1035 + 6 =

F 1006
G 1021
H 129
J 151
K None of these

Tips

If the right answer is not given, mark the space for "None of these."

The answer in an addition problem is always larger than the numbers being added.

Practice

1

20 + 17 + 8 =

A 25
B 35
C 45
D 47
E None of these

2

$$\begin{array}{r} 328 \\ +\ 261 \\ \hline \end{array}$$

F 589
G 587
H 547
J 689
K None of these

3

$$\begin{array}{r} 414 \\ 12 \\ 56 \\ +\ 25 \\ \hline \end{array}$$

A 451
B 4070
C 497
D 507
E None of these

4

$$\begin{array}{r} 2754 \\ +\ 4378 \\ \hline \end{array}$$

F 6023
G 632
H 7123
J 7132
K None of these

5

$$\begin{array}{r} \$28.95 \\ +\ 17.39 \\ \hline \end{array}$$

A $36.64
B $9.56
C $46.25
D $46.35
E None of these

6

$$\begin{array}{r} 19{,}576 \\ +\ 40{,}283 \\ \hline \end{array}$$

F 58,859
G 59,713
H 59,759
J 59,859
K None of these

7

$$\begin{array}{r} 4991 \\ 708 \\ +\ 2435 \\ \hline \end{array}$$

A 624
B 6134
C 8134
D 82,354
E None of these

8

79.63 + 24.30 =

F 103.93
G 103.33
H 93.93
J 93.33
K None of these

GO

ANSWER ROWS
A Ⓐ Ⓑ Ⓒ Ⓓ Ⓔ 1 Ⓐ Ⓑ Ⓒ Ⓓ Ⓔ 3 Ⓐ Ⓑ Ⓒ Ⓓ Ⓔ 5 Ⓐ Ⓑ Ⓒ Ⓓ Ⓔ 7 Ⓐ Ⓑ Ⓒ Ⓓ Ⓔ
B Ⓕ Ⓖ Ⓗ Ⓙ Ⓚ 2 Ⓕ Ⓖ Ⓗ Ⓙ Ⓚ 4 Ⓕ Ⓖ Ⓗ Ⓙ Ⓚ 6 Ⓕ Ⓖ Ⓗ Ⓙ Ⓚ 8 Ⓕ Ⓖ Ⓗ Ⓙ Ⓚ

9

$$\begin{array}{r} 1\frac{3}{8} \\ +\ 3\frac{4}{8} \\ \hline \end{array}$$

A $2\frac{1}{8}$
B $4\frac{1}{8}$
C $4\frac{7}{8}$
D $5\frac{3}{8}$
E None of these

10

29 + □ = 67

F 26
G 29
H 37
J 39
K None of these

11

$\frac{1}{6} + \frac{1}{3} =$

A $\frac{1}{36}$
B $\frac{2}{9}$
C $\frac{1}{2}$
D $\frac{1}{6}$
E None of these

12

$$\begin{array}{r} \$91.48 \\ +\ 9.14 \\ \hline \end{array}$$

F \$991.62
G \$100.62
H \$100.34
J \$90.60
K None of these

13

$$\begin{array}{r} \frac{2}{11} \\ +\ \frac{4}{11} \\ \hline \end{array}$$

A $\frac{6}{11}$
B $\frac{5}{11}$
C $\frac{6}{22}$
D $\frac{2}{22}$
E None of these

14

2.9 + 0.8 =

F 2.89
G 2.98
H 3.1
J 3.7
K None of these

15

$$\begin{array}{r} 1\frac{3}{7} \\ +\ 4\frac{4}{7} \\ \hline \end{array}$$

A 6
B $5\frac{6}{7}$
C $5\frac{1}{7}$
D $3\frac{1}{7}$
E None of these

16

67,035 + 12,201 =

F 55,234
G 78,236
H 79,254
J 79,236
K None of these

17

$\frac{3}{11} + \frac{8}{11} =$ □

A $\frac{5}{11}$
B $\frac{11}{22}$
C $\frac{9}{11}$
D 1
E None of these

18

33 + 78 =

F 101
G 111
H 118
J 128
K None of these

STOP

ANSWER ROWS 9 Ⓐ Ⓑ Ⓒ Ⓓ Ⓔ 11 Ⓐ Ⓑ Ⓒ Ⓓ Ⓔ 13 Ⓐ Ⓑ Ⓒ Ⓓ Ⓔ 15 Ⓐ Ⓑ Ⓒ Ⓓ Ⓔ 17 Ⓐ Ⓑ Ⓒ Ⓓ Ⓔ
10 Ⓕ Ⓖ Ⓗ Ⓙ Ⓚ 12 Ⓕ Ⓖ Ⓗ Ⓙ Ⓚ 14 Ⓕ Ⓖ Ⓗ Ⓙ Ⓚ 16 Ⓕ Ⓖ Ⓗ Ⓙ Ⓚ 18 Ⓕ Ⓖ Ⓗ Ⓙ Ⓚ

Example

Directions: Mark the space for the correct answer to each subtraction problem. Choose "NG" if the right answer is not given.

A

$$\begin{array}{r} 14 \\ -\ 11 \\ \hline \end{array}$$

A 25
B 32
C 4
D 3
E NG

B

$20 - 5 =$

F 14
G 21
H 25
J 4
K NG

Tips

If the right answer is not given, mark the space for "NG." This means "not given."

When you are not sure of an answer, check it by adding.

Practice

1

$$\begin{array}{r} 431 \\ -\ 267 \\ \hline \end{array}$$

A 236
B 264
C 166
D 164
E NG

2

$$\begin{array}{r} 9988 \\ -\ 2121 \\ \hline \end{array}$$

F 777
G 7877
H 12,109
J 7766
K NG

3

$$\begin{array}{r} 913 \\ -\ 68 \\ \hline \end{array}$$

A 981
B 845
C 1081
D 373
E NG

4

$$\begin{array}{r} 8.29 \\ -\ 2.24 \\ \hline \end{array}$$

F 6.25
G 10.53
H 6.05
J 82.45
K NG

5

$$\begin{array}{r} 3048 \\ -\ 695 \\ \hline \end{array}$$

A 3021
B 2353
C 3353
D 3653
E NG

6

$55.20 – $17.48 =

F $72.68
G $47.72
H $32.68
J $37.82
K NG

7

$$\begin{array}{r} 28.1 \\ -\ 26.9 \\ \hline \end{array}$$

A 1.2
B 2.2
C 55
D 1.19
E NG

8

$$\begin{array}{r} 62.26 \\ -\ 14.99 \\ \hline \end{array}$$

F 86.15
G 57.27
H 57.73
J 47.27
K NG

GO

ANSWER ROWS
A Ⓐ Ⓑ Ⓒ Ⓓ Ⓔ 1 Ⓐ Ⓑ Ⓒ Ⓓ Ⓔ 3 Ⓐ Ⓑ Ⓒ Ⓓ Ⓔ 5 Ⓐ Ⓑ Ⓒ Ⓓ Ⓔ 7 Ⓐ Ⓑ Ⓒ Ⓓ Ⓔ
B Ⓕ Ⓖ Ⓗ Ⓙ Ⓚ 2 Ⓕ Ⓖ Ⓗ Ⓙ Ⓚ 4 Ⓕ Ⓖ Ⓗ Ⓙ Ⓚ 6 Ⓕ Ⓖ Ⓗ Ⓙ Ⓚ 8 Ⓕ Ⓖ Ⓗ Ⓙ Ⓚ

9

$$\begin{array}{r} 3\frac{5}{8} \\ -\ 2\frac{4}{8} \\ \hline \end{array}$$

A $1\frac{1}{8}$
B $\frac{1}{8}$
C $5\frac{7}{8}$
D $1\frac{7}{8}$
E NG

10

$\frac{8}{9} - \frac{6}{9} =$

F $\frac{14}{9}$
G $1\frac{4}{9}$
H $\frac{1}{3}$
J $\frac{2}{9}$
K NG

11

$\frac{4}{4} - \frac{3}{4} =$

A $\frac{1}{4}$
B $\frac{2}{3}$
C $\frac{7}{4}$
D 1
E NG

12

$$\begin{array}{r} 5\frac{4}{9} \\ -\ \ \frac{2}{9} \\ \hline \end{array}$$

F $5\frac{1}{3}$
G $5\frac{2}{3}$
H $5\frac{2}{9}$
J $5\frac{1}{9}$
K NG

13

$$\begin{array}{r} \$87.95 \\ -\ 83.74 \\ \hline \end{array}$$

A $171.69
B $4.89
C $4.21
D $3.21
E NG

14

$$\begin{array}{r} \frac{15}{12} \\ -\ \frac{8}{12} \\ \hline \end{array}$$

F $\frac{7}{12}$
G $1\frac{3}{4}$
H $\frac{11}{12}$
J $\frac{1}{2}$
K NG

15

0.711 − 0.462 =

A 1.173
B 0.349
C 0.249
D 0.351
E NG

16

$\frac{3}{4} - \frac{1}{8} =$

F 1
G $\frac{1}{2}$
H $\frac{3}{8}$
J $\frac{5}{8}$
K NG

17

35 − 9 = □

A 16
B 34
C 25
D 27
E NG

18

$$\begin{array}{r} 9004 \\ -\ 2395 \\ \hline \end{array}$$

F 7391
G 6609
H 7609
J 6391
K NG

STOP

ANSWER ROWS

9 Ⓐ Ⓑ Ⓒ Ⓓ Ⓔ **12** Ⓕ Ⓖ Ⓗ Ⓙ Ⓚ **15** Ⓐ Ⓑ Ⓒ Ⓓ Ⓔ **17** Ⓐ Ⓑ Ⓒ Ⓓ Ⓔ
10 Ⓕ Ⓖ Ⓗ Ⓙ Ⓚ **13** Ⓐ Ⓑ Ⓒ Ⓓ Ⓔ **16** Ⓕ Ⓖ Ⓗ Ⓙ Ⓚ **18** Ⓕ Ⓖ Ⓗ Ⓙ Ⓚ
11 Ⓐ Ⓑ Ⓒ Ⓓ Ⓔ **14** Ⓕ Ⓖ Ⓗ Ⓙ Ⓚ

Lesson 8 Multiplication

Example

Directions: Mark the space for the correct answer to each multiplication problem. Choose "NH" if the right answer is not given.

A

$2.06
x 7

A $10.42
B $14.67
C $9.06
D $14.76
E NH

B

34 x 8 =

F 272
G 256
H 84
J 42
K NH

Tips

If the right answer is not given, mark the space for "NH." This means "not here."

Be sure to align numbers correctly when you multiply, especially during intermediate steps.

Practice

1

60
x 30

A 3600
B 1800
C 180
D 90
E NH

2

3.9 x 1.4 =

F 31.94
G 5.3
H 5.46
J 54.6
K NH

3

466
x 8

A 324,848
B 3266
C 32,488
D 3728
E NH

4

6 x 7 x 3 =

F 42
G 123
H 673
J 16
K NH

5

25 x 202 =

A 2252
B 5050
C 25,202
D 50,050
E NH

6

338
x 41

F 12,858
G 13,858
H 1385
J 1358
K NH

7

7 x ☐ = 504

A 702
B 77
C 7.2
D 72
E NH

8

5721
x 9

F 5730
G 59,489
H 51,489
J 51,389
K NH

STOP

ANSWER ROWS
A Ⓐ Ⓑ Ⓒ Ⓓ Ⓔ 1 Ⓐ Ⓑ Ⓒ Ⓓ Ⓔ 3 Ⓐ Ⓑ Ⓒ Ⓓ Ⓔ 5 Ⓐ Ⓑ Ⓒ Ⓓ Ⓔ 7 Ⓐ Ⓑ Ⓒ Ⓓ Ⓔ
B Ⓕ Ⓖ Ⓗ Ⓙ Ⓚ 2 Ⓕ Ⓖ Ⓗ Ⓙ Ⓚ 4 Ⓕ Ⓖ Ⓗ Ⓙ Ⓚ 6 Ⓕ Ⓖ Ⓗ Ⓙ Ⓚ 8 Ⓕ Ⓖ Ⓗ Ⓙ Ⓚ

Lesson 9 Division

Example

Directions: Mark the space for the correct answer to each division problem. Choose "N" if the right answer is not given.

A

$6\overline{)36}$

A 42
B 7
C 6
D N

B

65 ÷ 8 =

F 8
G 8 R1
H 9
J N

Tips

You can check your answers in a division problem by multiplying your answer by either the dividend or divisor.

If the right answer is not given, mark the space for "N." This means the answer is not given.

Practice

1

217 ÷ 7 =

A 41
B 210
C 31
D N

2

$58\overline{)406}$

F 81
G 81 R1
H 8
J N

3

39 ÷ 3 =

A 13
B 393
C 42
D N

4

$4\overline{)91}$

F 21 R3
G 23
H 12 R3
J N

5

$8\overline{)2729}$

A 330 R8
B 441
C 341 R1
D N

6

6519 ÷ 3 =

F 2173
G 2106 R1
H 9519
J N

7

$17\overline{)4658}$

A 273 R4
B 274
C 28
D N

8

126 ÷ 9 =

F 117
G 14
H 41
J N

STOP

ANSWER ROWS
A Ⓐ Ⓑ Ⓒ Ⓓ 1 Ⓐ Ⓑ Ⓒ Ⓓ 3 Ⓐ Ⓑ Ⓒ Ⓓ 5 Ⓐ Ⓑ Ⓒ Ⓓ 7 Ⓐ Ⓑ Ⓒ
B Ⓕ Ⓖ Ⓗ Ⓙ 2 Ⓕ Ⓖ Ⓗ Ⓙ 4 Ⓕ Ⓖ Ⓗ Ⓙ 6 Ⓕ Ⓖ Ⓗ Ⓙ 8 Ⓕ Ⓖ Ⓗ

Lesson 10 Test Yourself

Examples

Directions: Read and work each problem. Mark the space for the correct answer to each problem. Choose "None of these" if the right answer is not given.

E1

48 ÷ 12 =

A 8
B 12
C 4
D 6
E None of these

E2

14 − 1 =

F 4
G 1
H 12
J 11
K None of these

1

22 x 9 =

A 199
B 198
C 31
D 1818
E None of these

2

$$\begin{array}{r} \$9.10 \\ +\ 0.24 \\ \hline \end{array}$$

F $8.34
G $8.86
H $9.25
J $9.35
K None of these

3

$$\begin{array}{r} 2.04 \\ -\ 0.6 \\ \hline \end{array}$$

A 2.2
B 2.64
C 1.34
D 1.44
E None of these

4

320 ÷ 4 =

F 80
G 324
H 2480
J 804
K None of these

5

298 − 19 =

A 318
B 317
C 279
D 281
E None of these

6

$$\begin{array}{r} 109 \\ 207 \\ 400 \\ +\ 505 \\ \hline \end{array}$$

F 221
G 122
H 1220
J 1221
K None of these

7

$3\overline{)6918}$

A 6315
B 3261
C 231
D 2303
E None of these

8

$\frac{1}{7} \times 7 =$

F 1
G 7
H 8
J 10
K None of these

9

$$\begin{array}{r} 266 \\ -\ 79 \\ \hline \end{array}$$

A 287
B 187
C 213
D 107
E None of these

10

210 + 46 + 8197 =

F 8407
G 845
H 8453
J 10,453
K None of these

GO

ANSWER ROWS
E1 Ⓐ Ⓑ Ⓒ Ⓓ Ⓔ 2 Ⓕ Ⓖ Ⓗ Ⓙ Ⓚ 5 Ⓐ Ⓑ Ⓒ Ⓓ Ⓔ 8 Ⓕ Ⓖ Ⓗ Ⓙ Ⓚ
E2 Ⓕ Ⓖ Ⓗ Ⓙ Ⓚ 3 Ⓐ Ⓑ Ⓒ Ⓓ Ⓔ 6 Ⓕ Ⓖ Ⓗ Ⓙ Ⓚ 9 Ⓐ Ⓑ Ⓒ Ⓓ Ⓔ
1 Ⓐ Ⓑ Ⓒ Ⓓ Ⓔ 4 Ⓕ Ⓖ Ⓗ Ⓙ Ⓚ 7 Ⓐ Ⓑ Ⓒ Ⓓ Ⓔ 10 Ⓕ Ⓖ Ⓗ Ⓙ Ⓚ

11

$\frac{3}{5} + \frac{1}{2} = \square$

A $1\frac{1}{10}$
B $\frac{4}{7}$
C 1
D $1\frac{1}{11}$
E None of these

12

$9 \times 3.7 =$

F 27.7
G 33
H 277
J 33.3
K None of these

13

$8.4 + 7.1 =$

A 15.5
B 11.9
C 3.7
D 1.3
E None of these

14

$7 \overline{)62}$

F 9
G 8
H 8 R6
J 6 R8
K None of these

15

$\frac{1}{9} + \frac{1}{3}$

A $\frac{1}{9}$
B $\frac{2}{9}$
C $\frac{4}{9}$
D $\frac{4}{3}$
E None of these

16

$1 - \frac{4}{11} =$

F $\frac{1}{7}$
G $\frac{1}{2}$
H $1\frac{4}{11}$
J $\frac{6}{11}$
K None of these

17

$2881 + 5376$

A 7257
B 8257
C 8267
D 8357
E None of these

18

$6000 - 3295 =$

F 3705
G 3295
H 2705
J 3815
K None of these

19

483×44

A 527
B 2125
C 21,255
D 21,208
E None of these

20

$976 \div 8 =$

F 122
G 121
H 112
J 98
K None of these

21 **For this problem, do not reduce your answer to lowest terms.**

$2\frac{1}{8} + 2\frac{1}{8}$

A $4\frac{1}{8}$
B $4\frac{2}{8}$
C 5
D $5\frac{9}{8}$
E None of these

STOP

ANSWER ROWS
11 Ⓐ Ⓑ Ⓒ Ⓓ Ⓔ 14 Ⓕ Ⓖ Ⓗ Ⓙ Ⓚ 17 Ⓐ Ⓑ Ⓒ Ⓓ Ⓔ 20 Ⓕ Ⓖ Ⓗ Ⓙ Ⓚ
12 Ⓕ Ⓖ Ⓗ Ⓙ Ⓚ 15 Ⓐ Ⓑ Ⓒ Ⓓ Ⓔ 18 Ⓕ Ⓖ Ⓗ Ⓙ Ⓚ 21 Ⓐ Ⓑ Ⓒ Ⓓ Ⓔ
13 Ⓐ Ⓑ Ⓒ Ⓓ Ⓔ 16 Ⓕ Ⓖ Ⓗ Ⓙ Ⓚ 19 Ⓐ Ⓑ Ⓒ Ⓓ Ⓔ

NUMBER RIGHT______

Lesson 11 Geometry

Example

Directions: Find the correct answer to each geometry problem. Mark the space for your choice.

A What is the volume of the shape on the right?

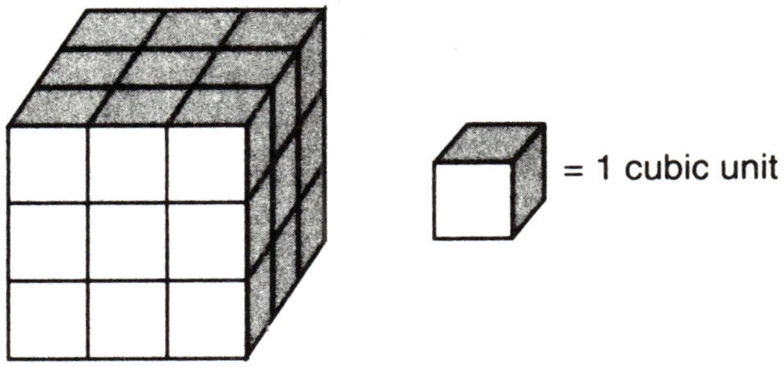

A 9 cubic units

B 18 cubic units

C 27 cubic units

D 81 cubic units

Tips

When you are not sure of an answer, eliminate the choices you know are wrong, then take your best guess.

Practice

1 How many pairs of lines below intersect?

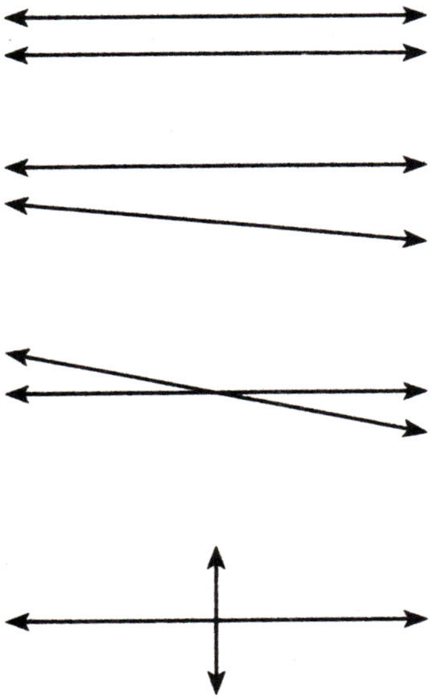

A one

B two

C three

D four

2 A drawing of the playground in Hallville is shown below. Which of these statements is true about the playground?

F The perimeter is 64 yards.

G The perimeter is 128 yards.

H The perimeter is less than 128 yards.

J The perimeter is more than 128 yards.

3 One edge of a cube is called a —

A line

B point

C face

D volume

GO

ANSWER ROWS **A** Ⓐ Ⓑ Ⓒ Ⓓ **1** Ⓐ Ⓑ Ⓒ Ⓓ **2** Ⓕ Ⓖ Ⓗ Ⓙ **3** Ⓐ Ⓑ Ⓒ Ⓓ

4 Two friends made up a code in which shapes stood for letters. Part of the code is shown below. Use the code to figure out what word is spelled by the shapes in the box.

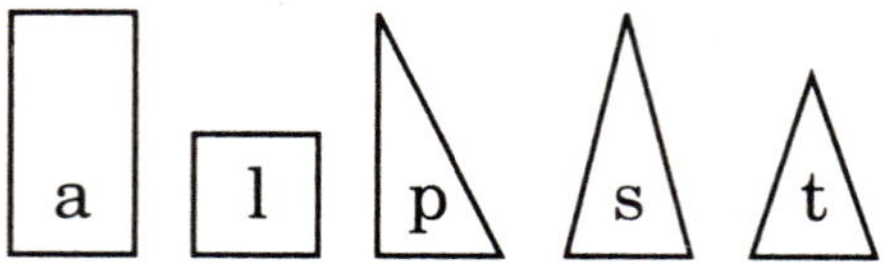

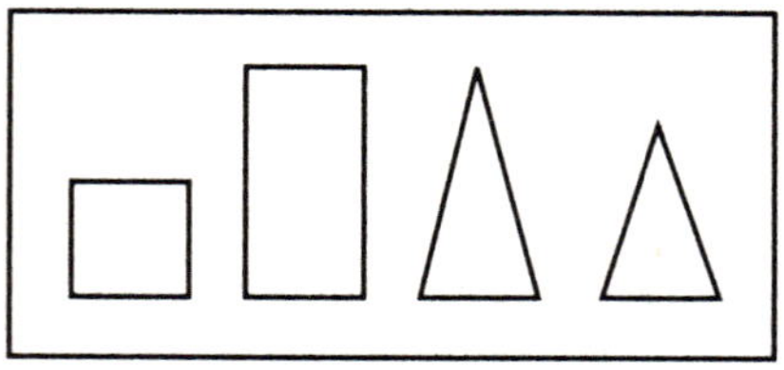

F tall

G salt

H last

J past

5 The circle below has a diameter of 20 units. Which line is 10 units long?

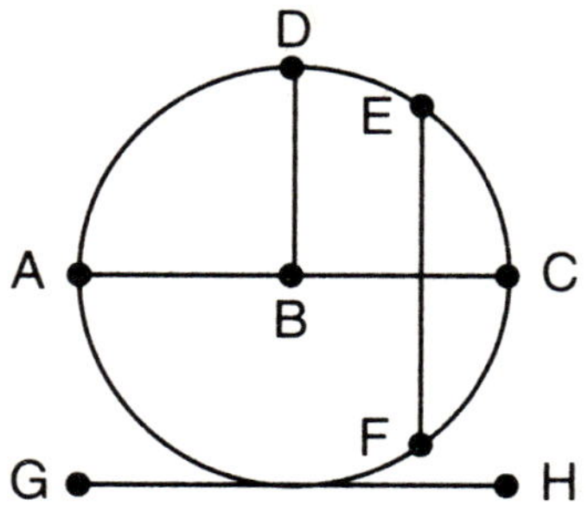

A $\overline{AC}$

B $\overline{BD}$

C $\overline{EF}$

D $\overline{GH}$

6 Which of these figures has no right angles?

F

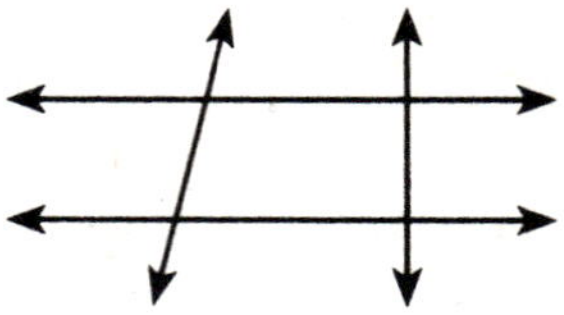

G

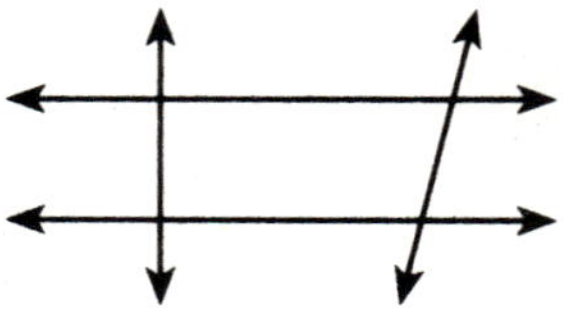

H

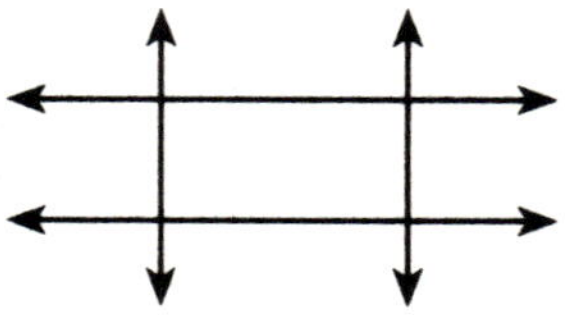

J

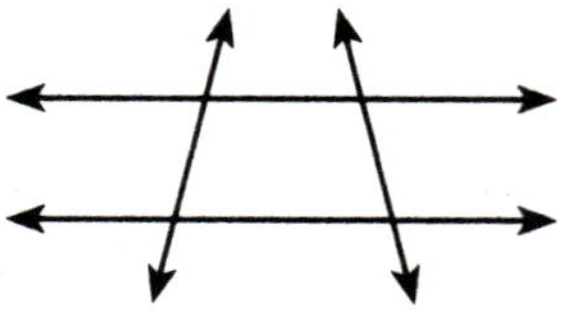

7 How can you compute the area of the figure below?

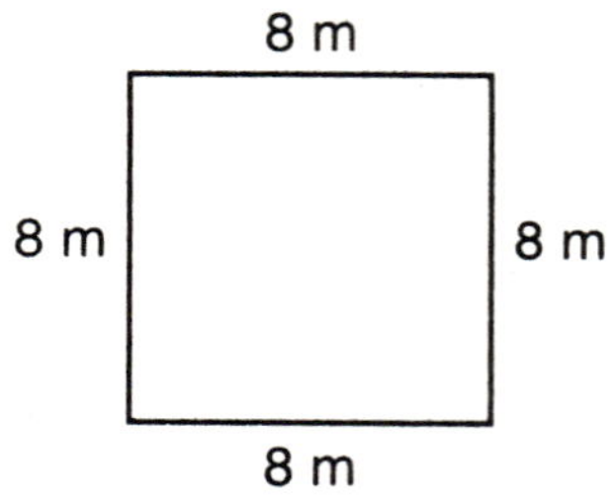

A 4m x 8m

B 8m x 8m

C 8m + 8m + 8m + 8m

D (2 x 8) + (2 x 8)

8 A railroad car is shaped most like a —

F triangular prism

G rectangular prism

H cube

J sphere

GO

ANSWER ROWS 4 Ⓕ Ⓖ Ⓗ Ⓙ 5 Ⓐ Ⓑ Ⓒ Ⓓ 6 Ⓕ Ⓖ Ⓗ Ⓙ 7 Ⓐ Ⓑ Ⓒ Ⓓ 8 Ⓕ Ⓖ Ⓗ Ⓙ

9 Which numbered triangle is similar to triangle A?

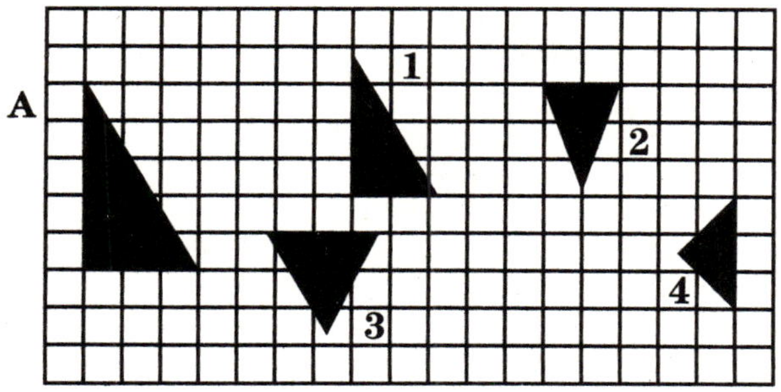

A triangle 1

B triangle 2

C triangle 3

D triangle 4

10 Which of these is an acute angle?

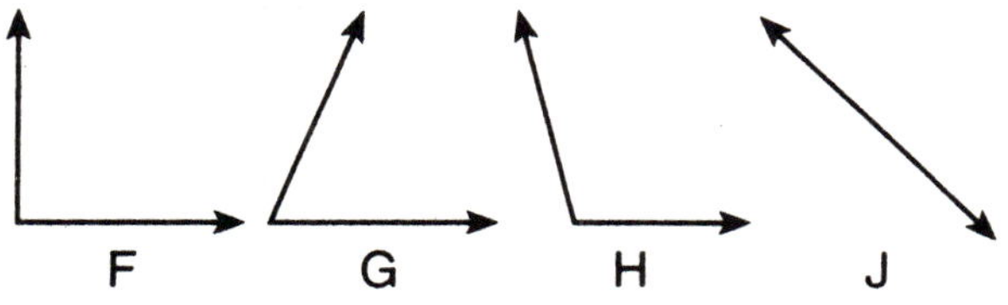

F F

G G

H H

J J

11 The area of the figure below is —

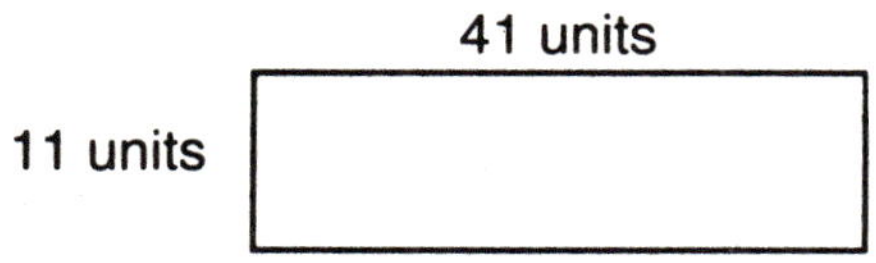

A 52 square units

B 104 square units

C 411 square units

D 451 square units

12 Which of these shows a ray?

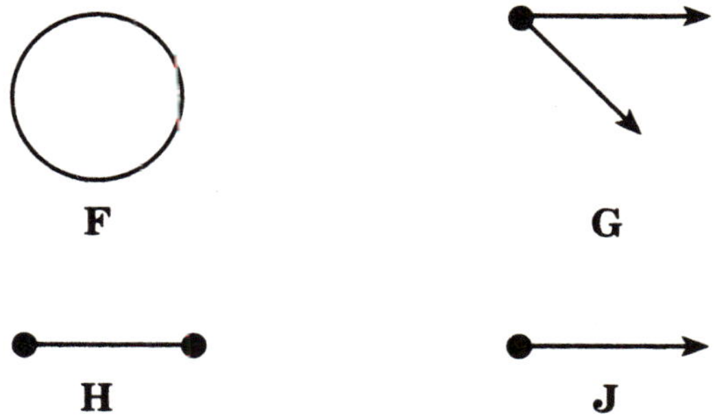

13 Which statement is true about the shape below?

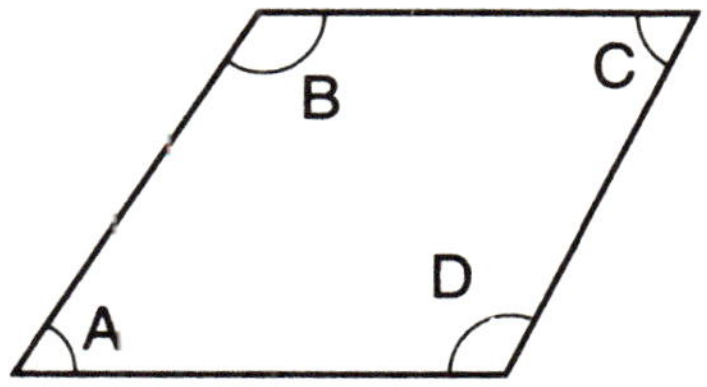

A Angles A and C are right angles.

B Angles A and C are obtuse angles.

C Angles B and D are obtuse angles.

D Angles B and D are acute angles.

14 What is the area of a desk that is 30 inches long by 25 inches wide?

F 55 square inches

G 750 square inches

H 110 square inches

J 3025 square inches

15 Which of these shows a line of symmetry?

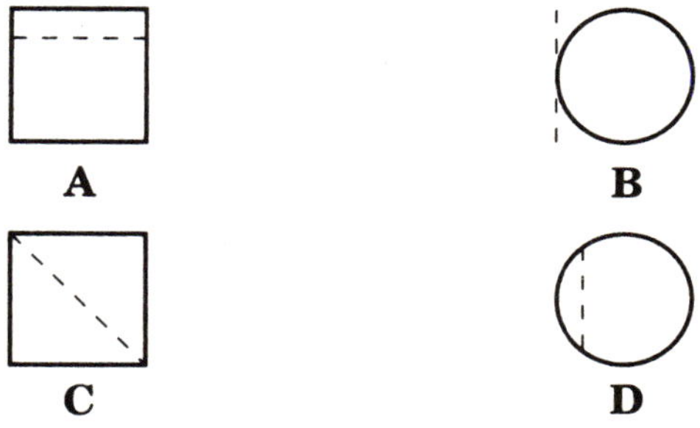

GO

ANSWER ROWS 9 Ⓐ Ⓑ Ⓒ Ⓓ 11 Ⓐ Ⓑ Ⓒ Ⓓ 13 Ⓐ Ⓑ Ⓒ Ⓓ 15 Ⓐ Ⓑ Ⓒ Ⓓ
10 Ⓕ Ⓖ Ⓗ Ⓙ 12 Ⓕ Ⓖ Ⓗ Ⓙ 14 Ⓕ Ⓖ Ⓗ Ⓙ

16 Which pair of shapes is congruent?

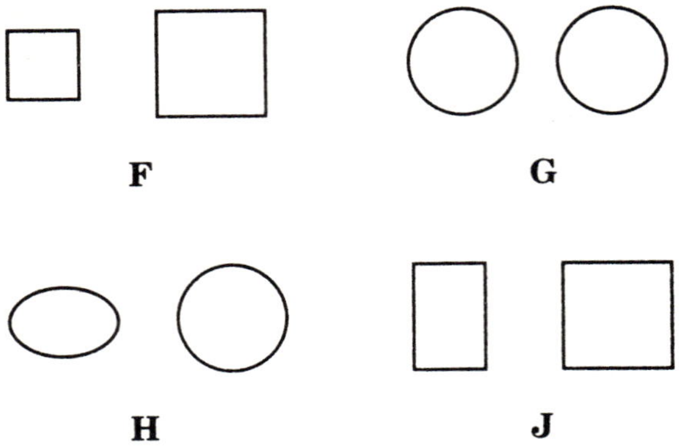

17 Which of these lines are parallel?

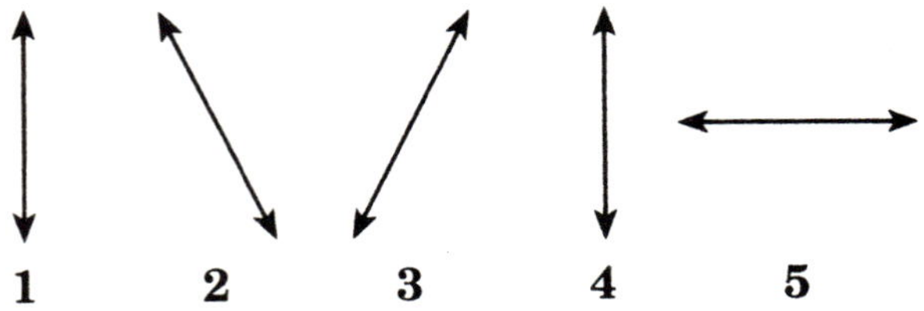

A 1 and 5

B 1 and 4

C 2 and 3

D 2 and 5

18 A picture is 12 inches wide by 16 inches long. How much wood will you need to make a frame for the picture?

F 56 inches

G 48 inches

H 192 inches

J 28 inches

19 How many corners does a cube have?

A 4

B 6

C 7

D 8

20 What is the perimeter of this shape?

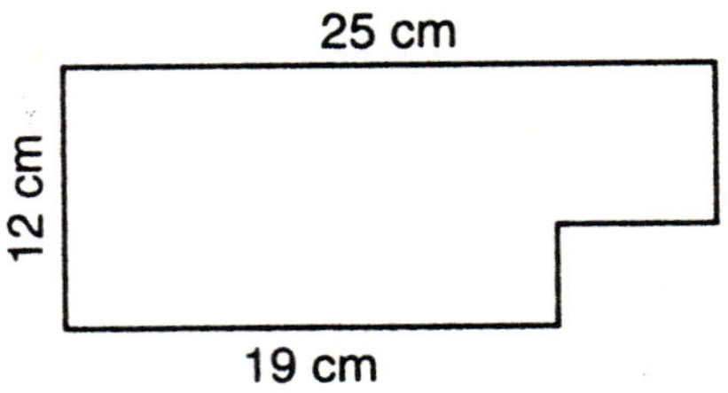

F 56 cm

G 300 cm

H 74 cm

J It cannot be determined.

21 Which of these figures shows perpendicular line segments?

A 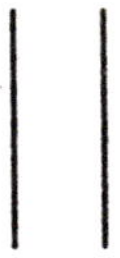

B 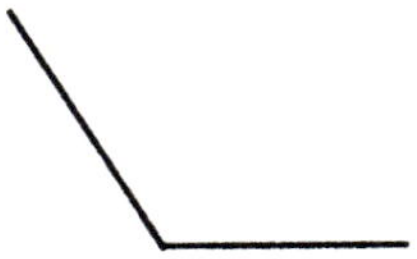

C 

D 

22 The distance around a triangular field is 1440 yards. The longest side is 600 yards and the shortest side is 360 yards. What is the length of the remaining side of the field?

F 400 yards

G 960 yards

H 480 yards

J 1440 yards

STOP

ANSWER ROWS 16 Ⓕ Ⓖ Ⓗ Ⓙ 18 Ⓕ Ⓖ Ⓗ Ⓙ 20 Ⓕ Ⓖ Ⓗ Ⓙ 22 Ⓕ Ⓖ Ⓗ Ⓙ

17 Ⓐ Ⓑ Ⓒ Ⓓ 19 Ⓐ Ⓑ Ⓒ Ⓓ 21 Ⓐ Ⓑ Ⓒ Ⓓ

Lesson 12 Measurement

Example

Directions: Find the correct answer to each measurement problem. Mark the space for your choice.

A How many inches are in 4 feet?

A 12 inches
B 48 inches
C 24 inches
D 40 inches

B Which of these statements is true?

F 12 quarters = $2.00
G 10 quarters = $2.00
H 20 nickels = $2.00
J 20 dimes = $2.00

Tips

You can solve some problems without computing. For these problems, it is especially important to look for key words, numbers, and figures to help you find the correct answer.

If you work on scrap paper, transfer numbers carefully and perform the correct operation.

Practice

1 Juanita is flying to her grandfather's house. The flight will take 4 hours. If the plane leaves at 6:30, which of these clocks shows the time the plane will land?

A

B

C

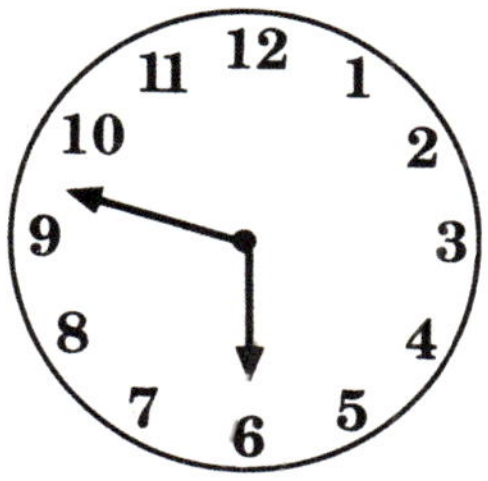

D

2 Which of these would best be measured in kilometers?

F The height of an average house
G The length of a large animal
H The height of a young tree
J The length of a long lake

3 Which of these measures is the largest?

A 10 pints
B 2 gallons
C 5 quarts
D 12 cups

4 12 meters =

F 1200 centimeters
G 120 centimeters
H 1.2 kilometers
J 0.12 kilometers

GO

ANSWER ROWS
A Ⓐ Ⓑ Ⓒ Ⓓ **1** Ⓐ Ⓑ Ⓒ Ⓓ **3** Ⓐ Ⓑ Ⓒ Ⓓ
B Ⓕ Ⓖ Ⓗ Ⓙ **2** Ⓕ Ⓖ Ⓗ Ⓙ **4** Ⓕ Ⓖ Ⓗ Ⓙ

5 When Tony arrived at the zoo, it was 9:15. He spent 2 hours and 30 minutes at the zoo and then met some friends for lunch. They spent 20 minutes in the cafeteria and then went to see the dolphin show. What time did Tony meet his friends for lunch?

A 11:15

B 9:35

C 12:05

D 11:45

6 Diana has $1.25 in coins. She has 3 quarters, 2 dimes, and the rest in nickels. How many nickels does Diana have?

F 6

G 5

H 7

J 3

7 About how long is this drawing of a carrot?

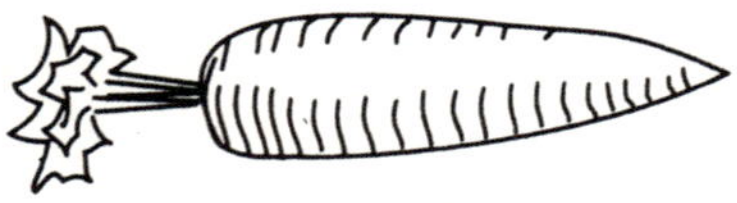

A 0.5 feet

B 0.5 yards

C 5 centimeters

D 5 inches

8 A broken pipe in a factory is leaking water at the rate of 2 pints per hour. It leaks for 2 days before it can be repaired. How many gallons of water were lost because of the leak?

F 96 gallons

G 12 gallons

H 4 gallons

J 24 gallons

9 Which of these is closest to the length of the line above this ruler?

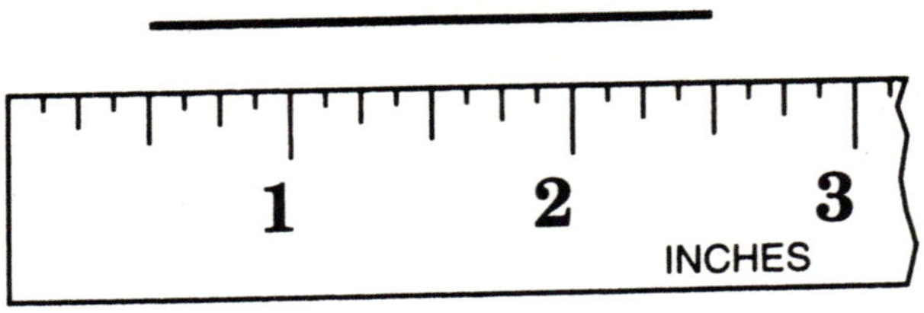

A $2\frac{1}{4}$ inches

B 2 inches

C $1\frac{1}{2}$ inches

D 1 inch

10 Which of these statements is true?

F 16 days is more than 3 weeks

G 2 days = 44 hours

H 6 weeks = 42 days

J 1 week is less than 100 hours

11 What temperature is shown on this thermometer?

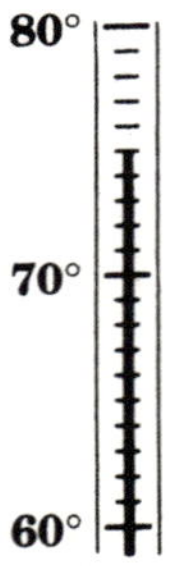

A 84°

B 76°

C 85°

D 75°

GO

ANSWER ROWS 5 Ⓐ Ⓑ Ⓒ Ⓓ 7 Ⓐ Ⓑ Ⓒ Ⓓ 9 Ⓐ Ⓑ Ⓒ Ⓓ 11 Ⓐ Ⓑ Ⓒ Ⓓ

6 Ⓕ Ⓖ Ⓗ Ⓙ 8 Ⓕ Ⓖ Ⓗ Ⓙ 10 Ⓕ Ⓖ Ⓗ Ⓙ

12 How long is one side of the cube shown below?

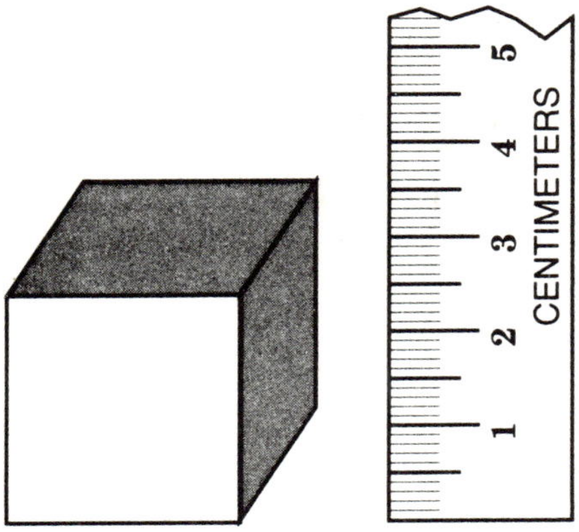

F 1.5 cm

G 2.5 cm

H 4 cm

J 3.5 cm

13 The temperature of a liquid is shown below. The liquid was heated so the temperature rose 65°. What was the temperature of the heated liquid?

A 96.5°

B 163°

C 104°

D 161.5°

14 About how high is a two-story building?

F 20 yards

G 20 inches

H 20 feet

J 20 meters

15 Juliana and Alexander began their bike ride at 10:00. They rode for about 6 hours and 30 minutes. Which clock shows what time they finished their ride?

A

B

C

D

16 Mt. Everest is about 10,000 yards high. How many miles is this?

F between 5 and 6 miles

G between 4 and 5 miles

H less than 4 miles

J more than 6 miles

17 Scottie and Brenda were on a trip to Europe with the school chorus. They went into a store and wanted to buy juice. What size bottle of juice were they most likely to find in the store?

A 100 milliliter

B 1000 liter

C 1 liter

D 1 milliliter

GO

18 A bus driver starts at midnight and works for 5 hours. He takes a break for an hour and then works 3 more hours. What fraction of a day does he work?

F $\frac{1}{3}$

G $\frac{3}{5}$

H $\frac{2}{8}$

J $\frac{1}{8}$

19 What time will this clock show in 35 minutes?

A 3:39

B 3:35

C 3:55

D 4:05

20 The container below holds one gallon of liquid when it is full. How much liquid is in the container now?

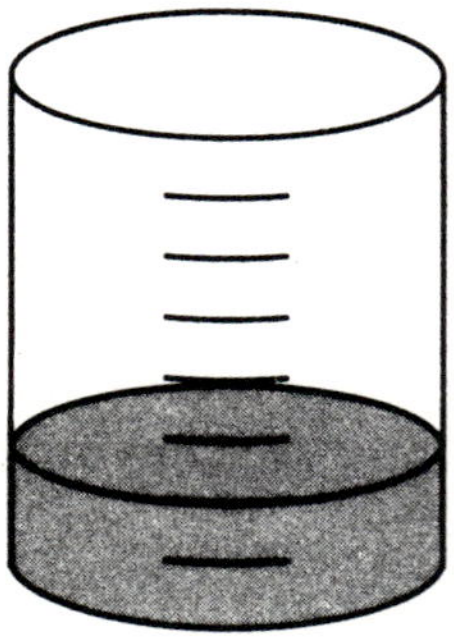

F 2 quarts

G 0.5 gallons

H 3 pints

J 1 quart

21 1 gram =

A 1000 kilograms

B 0.001 kilogram

C 0.1 kilogram

D 0.01 kilogram

22 Suppose you had 10 quarters and spent $1.60 for a burger. How much would you have left?

F $2.40

G $.40

H $1.90

J $.90

23 About how long is this whistle?

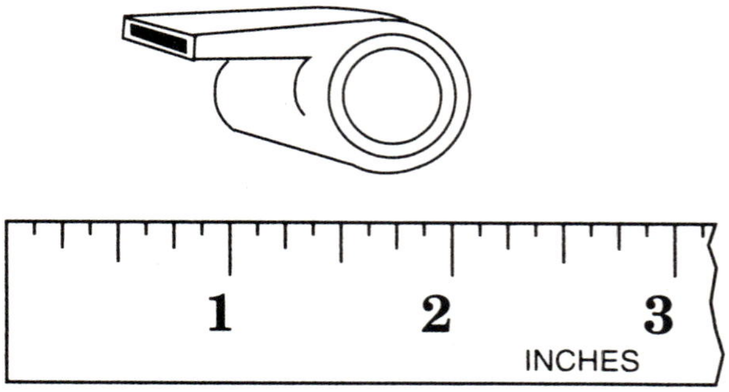

A $\frac{1}{2}$ inch

B $\frac{3}{4}$ inch

C $1\frac{1}{2}$ inches

D $2\frac{1}{2}$ inches

24 Math class starts at 9:15. It lasts for 50 minutes. Halfway through the class, the teacher will give the students a quiz. What time will they take the quiz?

F 9:40

G 10:05

H 9:50

J 10:10

STOP

ANSWER ROWS 18 Ⓕ Ⓖ Ⓗ Ⓙ 20 Ⓕ Ⓖ Ⓗ Ⓙ 22 Ⓕ Ⓖ Ⓗ Ⓙ 24 Ⓕ Ⓖ Ⓗ Ⓙ

19 Ⓐ Ⓑ Ⓒ Ⓓ 21 Ⓐ Ⓑ Ⓒ Ⓓ 23 Ⓐ Ⓑ Ⓒ Ⓓ

Example

Directions: Find the correct answer to each problem. Mark the space for your choice.

A A weekly bus pass costs $6.30. What is the cost per day if you ride the bus 5 days?

A $1.26
B $.90
C $1.30
D Not Given

B There are 15 girls in a class and 10 boys. What is the ratio of girls to boys?

F $\frac{1}{5}$
G $\frac{2}{5}$
H $\frac{2}{3}$
J Not Given

Tips

Read the question carefully. Look for key words, numbers, pictures, and figures. If necessary, work the problem on scratch paper.

Be sure to consider all the answer choices. Rework a problem if your answer is not one of the choices.

Practice

1 Lucas spent $6.00 for socks and $1.25 for shoe laces. How much did he spend all together?

A $6.25
B $4.75
C $7.25
D Not Given

2 The graph below shows how students responded to a question about the school cafeteria. If there were 600 students in the school, how many of them were "very satisfied" with the food in the cafeteria?

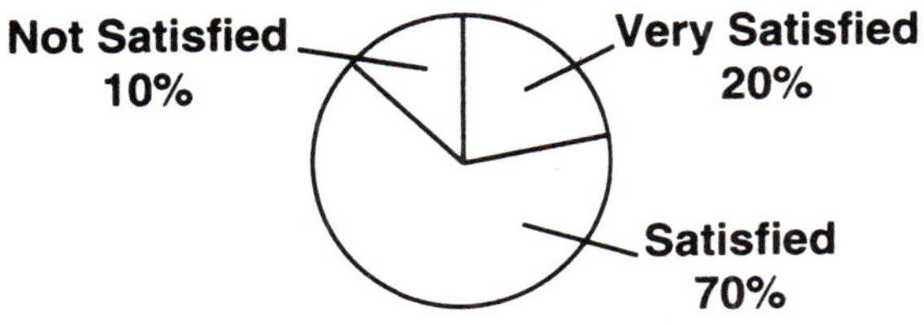

F 20
G 100
H 120
J Not Given

3 Charlene rode her bike 16 miles on Saturday and 30 miles on Sunday. How many more miles did she ride on Sunday?

A 46
B 4
C 16
D Not Given

4 On Saturday, Charlene's friend Allen rode with her. In addition to riding 16 miles with Charlene, he rode to and from his house to Charlene's. The distance from Allen's house to Charlene's is 2 miles. How far did Allen ride all together on Saturday?

F 20 miles
G 18 miles
H 12 miles
J Not Given

GO

ANSWER ROWS
A Ⓐ Ⓑ Ⓒ Ⓓ 1 Ⓐ Ⓑ Ⓒ Ⓓ 3 Ⓐ Ⓑ Ⓒ Ⓓ
B Ⓕ Ⓖ Ⓗ Ⓙ 2 Ⓕ Ⓖ Ⓗ Ⓙ 4 Ⓕ Ⓖ Ⓗ Ⓙ

Use this graph to answer questions 5 through 7.

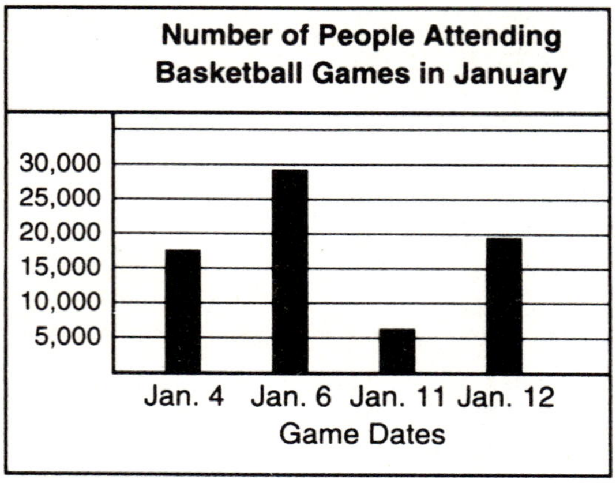

5 On which date was attendance at a game closest to 15,000?

A Jan. 12
B Jan. 4
C Jan. 11
D Not Given

6 How many more people attended the Jan. 6 game than the Jan. 12 game?

F 10,000
G 5,000
H 2,000
J Not Given

7 On one of the dates, a snow storm prevented many people from going to the game. On which date did the storm occur?

A Jan. 6
B Jan. 12
C Jan. 4
D Not Given

8 A family wants to meet friends who will arrive at the airport at 6:00 PM. What information do they need to leave the house in order to be at the airport on time?

F The time the flight takes off.
G How long the flight is.
H How long it takes to get to the airport.
J Not Given

The table below shows the cost of different size boxes. Use the table to answer questions 9 through 11.

10" x 12" x 24"	$2.50
12" x 14" x 24"	$3.00
12" x 12" x 12"	$2.00
14" x 14" x 16"	$2.50
18" x 18" x 30"	$4.00

9 What is the price difference between the cheapest and most expensive boxes?

A $4.00
B $2.00
C $2.50
D Not Given

10 Suppose you had a gift with dimensions 11" x 13" x 15". What is the least expensive box you could use to package your gift?

F 12″ x 14″ x 24″
G 12″ x 12″ x 12″
H 14″ x 14″ x 16″
J Not Given

11 How many boxes could hold a 17" long toy?

A 3
B 2
C 1
D Not Given

GO

Use the graph below to answer questions 12 through 15.

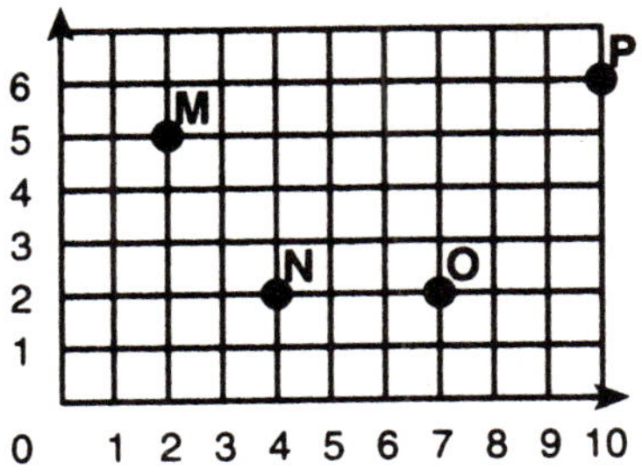

12 What point is at (7, 2)?

F M
G N
H P
J Not Given

13 What are the coordinates of point P?

A (10, 6)
B (6, 10)
C (10, 7)
D Not Given

14 If point N were moved up 2 units, what would its new coordinates be?

F (5, 4)
G (2, 2)
H (4, 4)
J Not Given

15 Suppose you connected points M-N, N-O, O-P, and P-M. How many sides would the figure you drew have?

A 2
B 4
C 8
D Not Given

16 There are 7 trucks in a garage. Each truck has 18 tires, and it takes 3 minutes to inspect each tire. Which number sentence shows how long it will take to inspect the tires on all the trucks?

F $(7 \times 18) \div 3 = \square$
G $7 \times 18 \times 3 = \square$
H $(7 \times 3) + 18 = \square$
J Not Given

Read this passage, then answer questions 17 and 18.

A sporting goods store is having a "blind luck" sale where you reach into a jar and pull out a piece of paper with the amount of your discount. In the jar are 4 pieces of paper with a discount of 40%, 6 pieces of paper with a discount of 30%, and 10 pieces of paper with a discount of 20%. All the merchandise in the store will be reduced by the amount of the discount on the paper you pull from the jar.

17 If you reached into the jar without looking, what are your chances of picking a piece of paper with a 40% discount?

A 1 out of 5
B 3 out of 10
C 4 out of 5
D Not Given

18 Suppose the athletic shoes you want cost $80 before the discount. The paper you pulled from the jar shows that you get a 30% discount. How much will the shoes cost after the discount?

F $50
G $64
H $24
J Not Given

GO

ANSWER ROWS 12 Ⓕ Ⓖ Ⓗ Ⓙ 14 Ⓕ Ⓖ Ⓗ Ⓙ 16 Ⓕ Ⓖ Ⓗ Ⓙ 18 Ⓕ Ⓖ Ⓗ Ⓙ
13 Ⓐ Ⓑ Ⓒ Ⓓ 15 Ⓐ Ⓑ Ⓒ Ⓓ 17 Ⓐ Ⓑ Ⓒ Ⓓ

This graph shows the changes in the depth of a river the day after a storm. Study the graph, then do numbers 19 through 21.

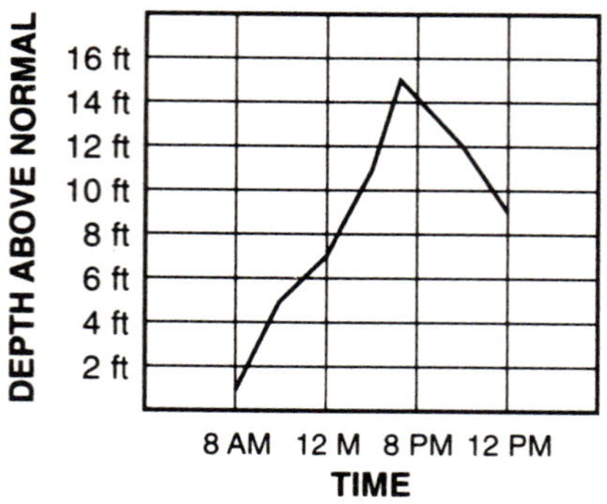

19 About what time did the river reach its highest point?

A about noon
B about 7 PM
C just after 8 PM
D Not Given

20 The river is 6 feet deep normally at the point where the measurement was taken. How deep was the river at 12 noon on the day after the storm?

F 13 feet
G 7 feet
H 14 feet
J Not Given

21 There is usually 10 feet of space between the river and a bridge that goes over it. During the storm, the river actually covered the bridge. About what time did the river reach the height of the bridge?

A around 12 midnight
B between 8 AM and 12 noon
C around 3 PM
D Not Given

22 The Red Bluff volleyball team won 14 games last season and lost half that many. How many games did they play in all?

F 7
G 21
H 28
J Not Given

23 What was the ratio of the games they won to the total number of games the Red Bluff volleyball team played?

A 2 to 1
B 1 to 2
C 2 to 3
D Not Given

24 To win a game, the Red Bluff team had to score 15 points. What was the total number of points they scored in the games they won?

F 315
G 214
H 201
J Not Given

25 The chart below shows how many points the Red Bluff team and their opponents scored in the championship playoffs. How many fewer points did Red Bluff score than their opponent in the first game they lost?

Red Bluff 15	Oakville 12
Red Bluff 15	Canyonlands 10
Silver Valley 15	Red Bluff 13
Red Bluff 15	West Slope 9
Rexville 15	Red Bluff 11

A 2
B 3
C 4
D Not Given

STOP

ANSWER ROWS 19 Ⓐ Ⓑ Ⓒ Ⓓ 21 Ⓐ Ⓑ Ⓒ Ⓓ 23 Ⓐ Ⓑ Ⓒ Ⓓ 25 Ⓐ Ⓑ Ⓒ Ⓓ
20 Ⓕ Ⓖ Ⓗ Ⓙ 22 Ⓕ Ⓖ Ⓗ Ⓙ 24 Ⓕ Ⓖ Ⓗ Ⓙ

Examples

Directions: Find the correct answer to each problem. Mark the space for your choice.

E1

About how much does a pair of athletic shoes weigh?

A 1 kiloliter
B 1 ounce
C 1 gram
D 1 kilogram

E2

Two lines that intersect to form a right angle are said to be —

F parallel
G perpendicular
H congruent
J similar

1 Which two angles are congruent?

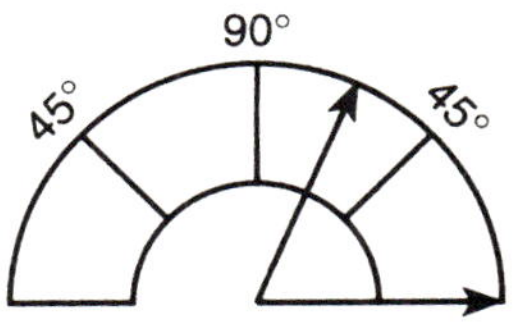

A

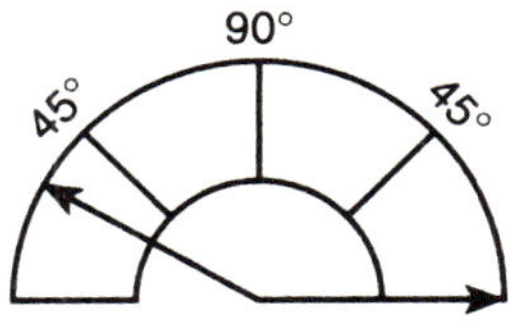

B

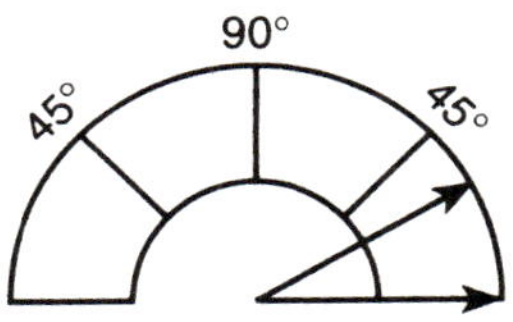

C

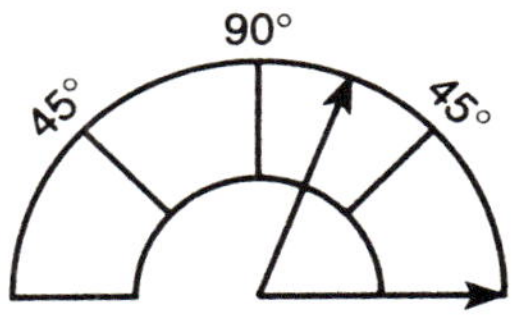

D

A C and A
B B and C
C A and B
D A and D

2 What is the area of this square?

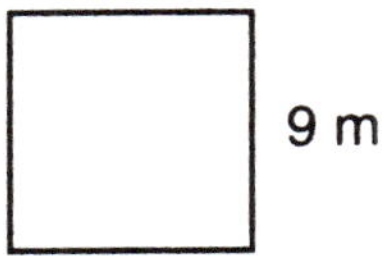

F 81 cm^2
G 36 cm^2
H 18 cm^2
J 3 cm^2

3 Three schools are going to be joined to form one larger school. The new school will have 1248 students. What was the average number of students in the three schools before they were joined?

A 448
B 1251
C 416
D 3744

4 The figure below is a rough sketch of the new school. If you walked around the school, about how far would you go?

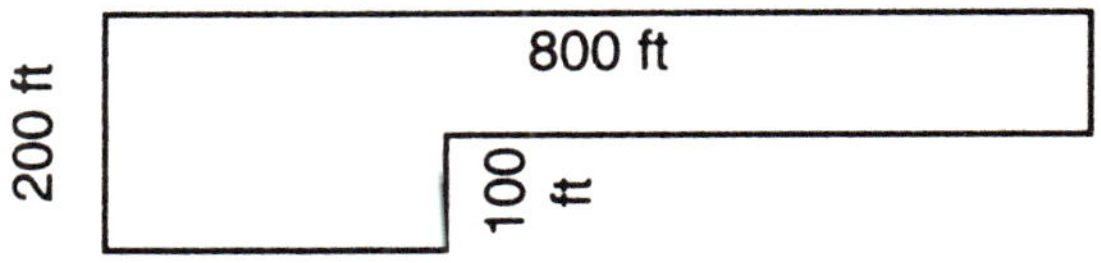

F 1100 ft
G 2000 ft
H 1200 ft
J 160,000 ft

5 What information would you need to find the number of girls and boys in the school?

A The ratio of girls to boys
B The average age of the girls and boys
C The range of grades in the school
D The size of each of the schools

GO

6 This clock shows the time a train arrived at a station. The train loaded passengers for 10 minutes and then continued to the next station. The trip to the next station took 35 minutes. What time did the train arrive at the next station?

F 2:30

G 2:05

H 2:40

J 2:35

7 An auto mechanic earns $19 an hour. She works 8 hours a day. Which number sentence shows how to find how much she earns in a day?

A 19 + 8 = ☐

B 19 – 8 = ☐

C 19 x 8 = ☐

D 19 + 8 = ☐

8 What is the volume of this figure?

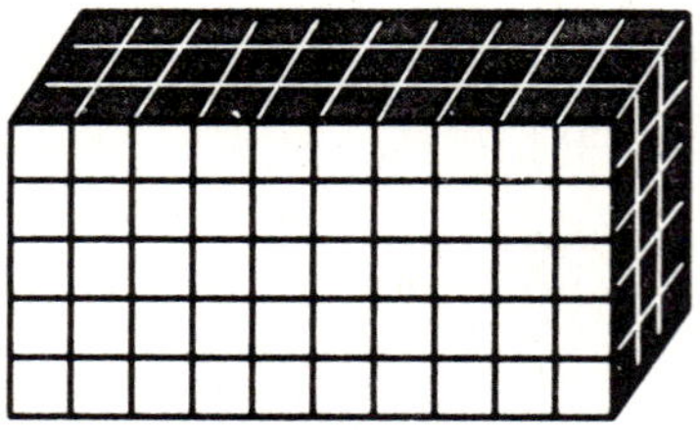

 = 1 cubic unit

F 150 cubic units

G 100 cubic units

H 53 cubic units

J 50 cubic units

9 A triangular field is enclosed with 568 meters of fence. Two sides of the field are the same length, 190 meters. What is the length of the third side?

A 190 meters

B 188 meters

C 168 meters

D 378 meters

The graph below is missing some important information. Even so, you can still interpret the results. Study the graph, then answer questions 10 and 11.

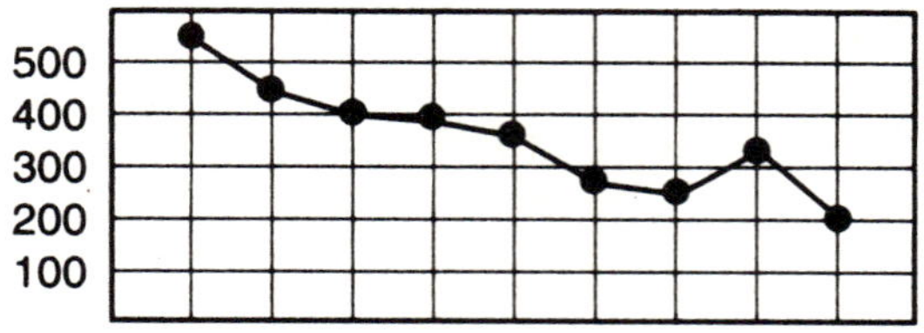

10 What is the difference in units between the highest and lowest values on the graph?

F 350 units

G 400 units

H 600 units

J 300 units

11 Which of the situations described below might the graph represent?

A The increase in weight in ounces of a cat being fed a special diet.

B The cost of a product that is becoming more expensive because of inflation.

C The enrollment of a school in which the number of students is growing slowly.

D The depth of water in centimeters of a pond that was slowly being filled in by natural causes.

GO

ANSWER ROWS 6 Ⓕ Ⓖ Ⓗ Ⓙ 8 Ⓕ Ⓖ Ⓗ Ⓙ 10 Ⓕ Ⓖ Ⓗ Ⓙ

7 Ⓐ Ⓑ Ⓒ Ⓓ 9 Ⓐ Ⓑ Ⓒ Ⓓ 11 Ⓐ Ⓑ Ⓒ Ⓓ

The chart below shows the price of different types of carpet and their installation costs. Study the chart, then do numbers 12 through 14.

Carpet and Installation Costs

Maker	Material	Price per sq.yd.	Installation Cost per sq. yd.
du Bois	Nylon	$6.50	$1.00
Marquee	Nylon	$7.50	$1.00
Howard	Wool	$15.00	$1.25
Mead	Wool	$17.25	$1.50
Corbett	Blend	$12.50	$1.00
Folsom	Blend	$28.00	*
Sindler	Blend	$25.50	$3.00

* Installation is included in price

12 What would the total cost be, including installation, to put Marquee carpet in a room that was 12 feet by 15 feet?

F $150

G $170

H $130

J $1170

13 Which of these installations would be most expensive?

A 10 sq. yds. of Folsom

B 10 sq. yds. of Sindler

C 12 sq. yds. of Howard

D 15 sq. yds. of du Bois

14 A carpet store is reducing the price of Mead carpet by $2.25, but the installation cost will remain the same. What will the total price be to install 360 square feet of carpet?

F $620

G $500

H $690

J $660

15 A recipe for trail mix calls for $\frac{3}{4}$ cup of raisins, $2\frac{3}{4}$ cups of granola, and $\frac{1}{2}$ cup of nuts. How much trail mix will this recipe make?

A $3\frac{3}{4}$ cups

B $3\frac{1}{4}$ cups

C $4\frac{3}{4}$ cups

D 4 cups

16 Suppose you had $6.50 in coins. Which of these groups of coins might you have?

F 60 dimes

G 26 quarters

H 35 nickels

J 15 half-dollars

17 Willie earned $24 on Tuesday, $36 on Wednesday, and $30 on Friday. What is the average amount he earned for the three days?

A $32

B $33

C $30

D $90

18 A box of nails contains about 125 nails. A case contains 12 boxes. A store owner has 4 cases and 7 boxes of nails. How many nails in all does the store owner have?

F 6000 nails

G 55 nails

H 2875 nails

J 6875 nails

GO

ANSWER ROWS 12 Ⓕ Ⓖ Ⓗ Ⓙ 14 Ⓕ Ⓖ Ⓗ Ⓙ 16 Ⓕ Ⓖ Ⓗ Ⓙ 18 Ⓕ Ⓖ Ⓗ Ⓙ
13 Ⓐ Ⓑ Ⓒ Ⓓ 15 Ⓐ Ⓑ Ⓒ Ⓓ 17 Ⓐ Ⓑ Ⓒ Ⓓ

Use this graph to answer questions 19 through 22.

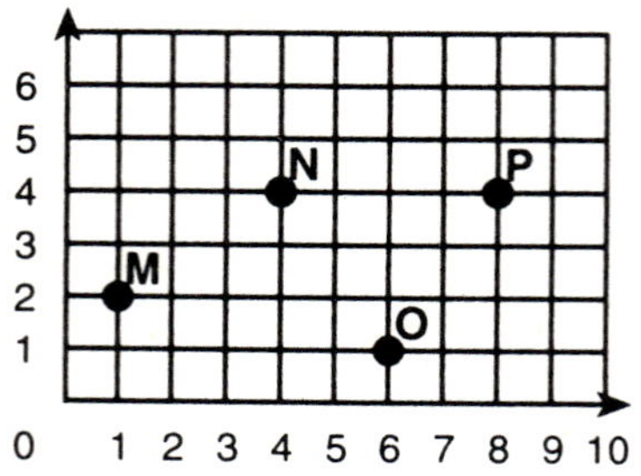

19 What point is at (4, 4)?

A M

B N

C O

D P

20 If you connected points N and P, P and O, and O and N, what figure would you form?

F a rectangle

G a square

H a triangle

J a trapezoid

21 How would you have to move to go from point N to point P?

A -4 units horizontally

B +4 units horizontally

C +2 units horizontally, -3 units vertically

D -3 units horizontally, -2 units vertically

22 Which two points are farthest from one another?

F M and O

G M and P

H N and P

J N and O

23 In which shape are all the corners right angles?

A triangle

B trapezoid

C rectangular prism

D pyramid

24 Which of these does not show a line of symmetry?

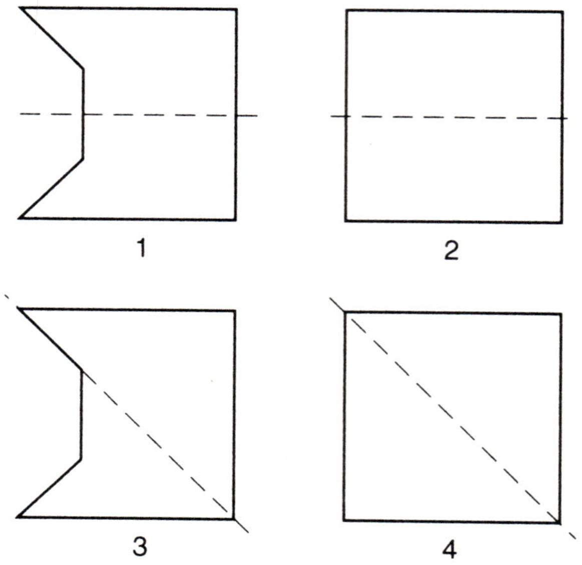

F 1

G 2

H 3

J 4

25 A bicycle race is 50 kilometers. How many meters is this?

A 5000 meters

B 500 meters

C 5100 meters

D 50,000 meters

STOP

ANSWER ROWS 19 Ⓐ Ⓑ Ⓒ Ⓓ 21 Ⓐ Ⓑ Ⓒ Ⓓ 23 Ⓐ Ⓑ Ⓒ Ⓓ 25 Ⓐ Ⓑ Ⓒ Ⓓ

20 Ⓕ Ⓖ Ⓗ Ⓙ 22 Ⓕ Ⓖ Ⓗ Ⓙ 24 Ⓕ Ⓖ Ⓗ Ⓙ

NUMBER RIGHT______

Name and Answer Sheet

To the Student:

These tests will give you a chance to put the tips you have learned to work.

A few last reminders…

- Be sure you understand all the directions before you begin each test. You may ask the teacher questions about the directions if you do not understand them.
- Work as quickly as you can during each test.
- When you change an answer, be sure to erase your first mark completely.
- You can guess at an answer or skip difficult items and go back to them later.
- Use the tips you have learned whenever you can.
- It is OK to be a little nervous. You may even do better.

Now that you have completed the lessons in this unit, you are on your way to scoring high!

STUDENT'S NAME

LAST | FIRST | MI

A B C D E F G H I J K L M N O P Q R S T U V W X Y Z

SCHOOL

TEACHER

FEMALE ◯ MALE ◯

BIRTHDATE

MONTH	DAY		YEAR	
JAN	0	0		0
FEB	1	1		1
MAR	2	2		2
APR	3	3		3
MAY		4		4
JUN		5	5	5
JUL		6	6	6
AUG		7	7	7
SEP		8	8	8
OCT		9	9	9
NOV				
DEC				

GRADE

3 4 5 6 7 8

PART 1 CONCEPTS

E1 Ⓐ Ⓑ Ⓒ Ⓓ	4 Ⓕ Ⓖ Ⓗ Ⓙ	9 Ⓐ Ⓑ Ⓒ Ⓓ	14 Ⓕ Ⓖ Ⓗ Ⓙ	18 Ⓕ Ⓖ Ⓗ Ⓙ	22 Ⓕ Ⓖ Ⓗ Ⓙ
E2 Ⓕ Ⓖ Ⓗ Ⓙ	5 Ⓐ Ⓑ Ⓒ Ⓓ	10 Ⓕ Ⓖ Ⓗ Ⓙ	15 Ⓐ Ⓑ Ⓒ Ⓓ	19 Ⓐ Ⓑ Ⓒ Ⓓ	23 Ⓐ Ⓑ Ⓒ Ⓓ
1 Ⓐ Ⓑ Ⓒ Ⓓ	6 Ⓕ Ⓖ Ⓗ Ⓙ	11 Ⓐ Ⓑ Ⓒ Ⓓ	16 Ⓕ Ⓖ Ⓗ Ⓙ	20 Ⓕ Ⓖ Ⓗ Ⓙ	24 Ⓕ Ⓖ Ⓗ Ⓙ
2 Ⓕ Ⓖ Ⓗ Ⓙ	7 Ⓐ Ⓑ Ⓒ Ⓓ	12 Ⓕ Ⓖ Ⓗ Ⓙ	17 Ⓐ Ⓑ Ⓒ Ⓓ	21 Ⓐ Ⓑ Ⓒ Ⓓ	25 Ⓐ Ⓑ Ⓒ Ⓓ
3 Ⓐ Ⓑ Ⓒ Ⓓ	8 Ⓕ Ⓖ Ⓗ Ⓙ	13 Ⓐ Ⓑ Ⓒ Ⓓ			

PART 2 COMPUTATION

E1 Ⓐ Ⓑ Ⓒ Ⓓ Ⓔ	3 Ⓐ Ⓑ Ⓒ Ⓓ Ⓔ	7 Ⓐ Ⓑ Ⓒ Ⓓ Ⓔ	11 Ⓐ Ⓑ Ⓒ Ⓓ Ⓔ	15 Ⓐ Ⓑ Ⓒ Ⓓ Ⓔ	19 Ⓐ Ⓑ Ⓒ Ⓓ Ⓔ
E2 Ⓕ Ⓖ Ⓗ Ⓙ Ⓚ	4 Ⓕ Ⓖ Ⓗ Ⓙ Ⓚ	8 Ⓕ Ⓖ Ⓗ Ⓙ Ⓚ	12 Ⓕ Ⓖ Ⓗ Ⓙ Ⓚ	16 Ⓕ Ⓖ Ⓗ Ⓙ Ⓚ	20 Ⓕ Ⓖ Ⓗ Ⓙ Ⓚ
1 Ⓐ Ⓑ Ⓒ Ⓓ Ⓔ	5 Ⓐ Ⓑ Ⓒ Ⓓ Ⓔ	9 Ⓐ Ⓑ Ⓒ Ⓓ Ⓔ	13 Ⓐ Ⓑ Ⓒ Ⓓ Ⓔ	17 Ⓐ Ⓑ Ⓒ Ⓓ Ⓔ	21 Ⓐ Ⓑ Ⓒ Ⓓ Ⓔ
2 Ⓕ Ⓖ Ⓗ Ⓙ Ⓚ	6 Ⓕ Ⓖ Ⓗ Ⓙ Ⓚ	10 Ⓕ Ⓖ Ⓗ Ⓙ Ⓚ	14 Ⓕ Ⓖ Ⓗ Ⓙ Ⓚ	18 Ⓕ Ⓖ Ⓗ Ⓙ Ⓚ	

PART 3 APPLICATIONS

E1 Ⓐ Ⓑ Ⓒ Ⓓ	4 Ⓕ Ⓖ Ⓗ Ⓙ	9 Ⓐ Ⓑ Ⓒ Ⓓ	14 Ⓕ Ⓖ Ⓗ Ⓙ	19 Ⓐ Ⓑ Ⓒ Ⓓ	24 Ⓕ Ⓖ Ⓗ Ⓙ
E2 Ⓕ Ⓖ Ⓗ Ⓙ	5 Ⓐ Ⓑ Ⓒ Ⓓ	10 Ⓕ Ⓖ Ⓗ Ⓙ	15 Ⓐ Ⓑ Ⓒ Ⓓ	20 Ⓕ Ⓖ Ⓗ Ⓙ	25 Ⓐ Ⓑ Ⓒ Ⓓ
1 Ⓐ Ⓑ Ⓒ Ⓓ	6 Ⓕ Ⓖ Ⓗ Ⓙ	11 Ⓐ Ⓑ Ⓒ Ⓓ	16 Ⓕ Ⓖ Ⓗ Ⓙ	21 Ⓐ Ⓑ Ⓒ Ⓓ	26 Ⓕ Ⓖ Ⓗ Ⓙ
2 Ⓕ Ⓖ Ⓗ Ⓙ	7 Ⓐ Ⓑ Ⓒ Ⓓ	12 Ⓕ Ⓖ Ⓗ Ⓙ	17 Ⓐ Ⓑ Ⓒ Ⓓ	22 Ⓕ Ⓖ Ⓗ Ⓙ	27 Ⓐ Ⓑ Ⓒ Ⓓ
3 Ⓐ Ⓑ Ⓒ Ⓓ	8 Ⓕ Ⓖ Ⓗ Ⓙ	13 Ⓐ Ⓑ Ⓒ Ⓓ	18 Ⓕ Ⓖ Ⓗ Ⓙ	23 Ⓐ Ⓑ Ⓒ Ⓓ	

Part 1 Concepts

Examples

Directions: Find the correct answer to each problem. Mark the space for your choice.

E1

What is the fastest way to add 7 to itself 4 times?

A Divide 7 by 4

B Subtract 4 from 7

C Multiply 7 times 4

D Add 4 and 7

E2

What are all the factors of the product of 6 times 2?

F 2, 3, 12

G 2, 6

H 2, 3, 4, 6

J 1, 2, 3, 4, 6, 12

1 Which of these has the same area shaded as Figure 1?

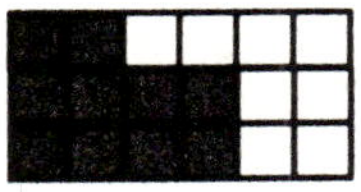

Figure 1

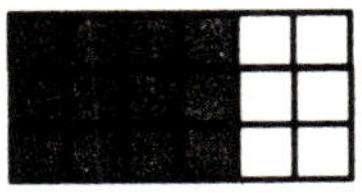

A

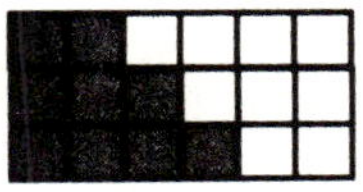

B

C

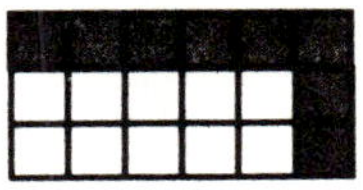

D

2 What should replace the box in the number sentence below?

81 ÷ 9 = (9 ÷ 3) x (9 ÷ □)

F 81

G 27

H 9

J 3

3 Which of these numbers is a common factor of 28 and 42?

A 6

B 7

C 8

D 4

4 Some students measured the weight of 3 rocks for a geology project. The rocks weighed 67 ounces, 78 ounces, and 62 ounces. If they rounded the weight of the rocks to the nearest 10 ounces and added them together, what number would they get?

F 200

G 210

H 190

J 220

5 A supermarket manager unloaded a cart of juice in 6-packs. She put 12 6-packs each on 4 shelves and had 5 6-packs left in the cart. How many 6-packs of juice were originally in the cart?

A 53 6-packs

B 21 6-packs

C 43 6-packs

D 64 6-packs

6 Which statement is true about the group of numbers below?

6, 9, 18, 42, 54, 75

F They can all be evenly divided by 5.

G They can all be evenly divided by 6.

H They can all be evenly divided by 3.

J They can all be evenly divided by 2.

7 Look at the table below. The numbers in column A are changed by the same rule to the numbers in column B. What are the missing numbers in column B?

A	B
24	18
22	16
20	
16	
10	4
8	2

A 14 and 10

B 14 and 8

C 15 and 10

D 12 and 8

8 Which of these numbers is greater than the Roman numeral IX?

F XI

G VIII

H V

J III

9 Sixteen thousand, nine hundred =

A 16,009

B 1609

C 16,000,900

D 16,900

10 If you shaded one more section of this figure, which decimal would it show?

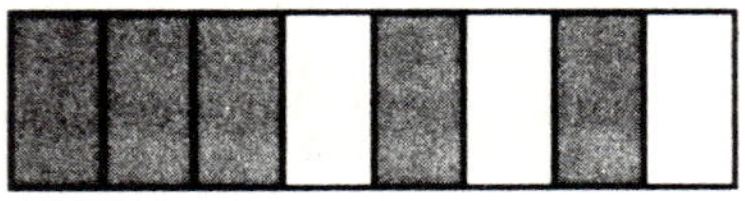

F 1.5

G 0.65

H 0.6

J 0.75

11 Which group of decimals is ordered from greatest to least?

A 4.849 4.603 4.471 4.236

B 4.169 4.207 4.325 4.564

C 4.503 4.172 4.673 4.489

D 4.002 4.993 4.285 4.714

12 Which number sentence goes with 5 x 8 = □?

F 8 x □ = 5

G 8 ÷ □ = 5

H □ ÷ 8 = 5

J □ − 8 = 5

13 Which of these is less than $\frac{1}{5}$?

A $\frac{2}{3}$

B $\frac{1}{10}$

C $\frac{1}{2}$

D $\frac{3}{4}$

14 Which of these is not another way to write the number 5276?

F 5000 + 200 + 70 + 6

G 5 thousands, 2 hundreds, 7 tens, 6 ones

H

1000s	100s	10s	1s
5	2	7	6

J five thousand, seventy-six

15 Which of these is a prime number?

A 28

B 22

C 23

D 33

16 In which of these does 1 have the greatest value?

F 705,736

G 810,427

H 321,845

J 120,967

17

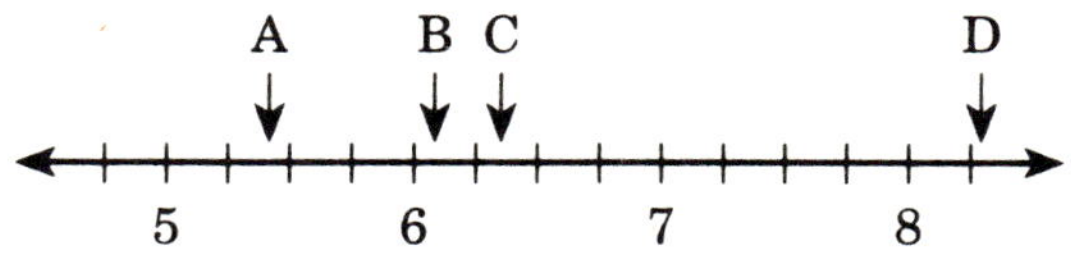

On the number line above, which arrow points most closely to 6.35?

A A

B B

C C

D D

18 $\sqrt{100}$

F 1

G 10

H 9

J 50

19 Suppose you replaced the 8 in the number 83,041 with a 1. How much smaller would the new number be?

A 10,000

B 70,000

C 1000

D 1

20 In which of these is y equal to 7?

F $15 \div 8 = y$

G $y + 15 = 8$

H $y + 8 = 15$

J $8 \times y = 15$

21 Which of these is odd and cannot be divided evenly by 7?

A 21

B 31

C 14

D 24

22 64 =

F 8^2

G 6^4

H 4^6

J 9^2

23 What symbol makes this number sentence true?

$$52 \square 4 = 13$$

A +

B –

C ÷

D x

24 Which of these is false?

F $\frac{1}{3} > \frac{1}{9}$

G $\frac{1}{4} > \frac{1}{2}$

H $\frac{1}{5} < \frac{1}{4}$

J $\frac{5}{6} < \frac{6}{5}$

25 What number should go in both boxes to make these number sentences true?

$$\square - 7 = 15$$
$$2 \times 11 = \square$$

A 85

B 12

C 21

D 22

STOP

Part 2 Computation

Examples **Directions:** Find the correct answer to each problem. Mark the space for your choice. Choose "None of these" if the correct answer is not given.

E1

$0.04 \times 40 =$

- **A** 16
- **B** 8
- **C** 0.44
- **D** 1.6
- **E** None of these

E2

$11\overline{)121}$

- **F** 110
- **G** 132
- **H** 12
- **J** 10
- **K** None of these

1

$9 \times 2 \times 6 =$

- **A** 926
- **B** 108
- **C** 72
- **D** 68
- **E** None of these

2

$$\begin{array}{r} \$12.09 \\ +\ 0.73 \\ \hline \end{array}$$

- **F** $13.63
- **G** $12.64
- **H** $12.79
- **J** $12.82
- **K** None of these

3

$$\begin{array}{r} 10.09 \\ -\ 0.9 \\ \hline \end{array}$$

- **A** 9.09
- **B** 9.11
- **C** 10.99
- **D** 9.99
- **E** None of these

4

$926 \div 7 =$

- **F** 123
- **G** 103 R5
- **H** 132
- **J** 132 R2
- **K** None of these

5

$2\frac{1}{2} - \frac{1}{3} =$

- **A** $2\frac{1}{6}$
- **B** 2
- **C** $1\frac{1}{3}$
- **D** $1\frac{1}{2}$
- **E** None of these

6

$$\begin{array}{r} 64 \\ 733 \\ 3 \\ +\ 521 \\ \hline \end{array}$$

- **F** 800
- **G** 736
- **H** 1318
- **J** 1321
- **K** None of these

7

$9\overline{)8298}$

- **A** 922
- **B** 1298
- **C** 7398
- **D** 911
- **E** None of these

8

$\frac{1}{2} \times 22 =$

- **F** 1
- **G** 11
- **H** 10
- **J** 12
- **K** None of these

9

$$\begin{array}{r} 6\frac{1}{2} \\ +\ 4\frac{1}{8} \\ \hline \end{array}$$

- **A** $2\frac{3}{8}$
- **B** $10\frac{5}{8}$
- **C** $10\frac{1}{8}$
- **D** $11\frac{1}{8}$
- **E** None of these

10

$100 + 72 + 9933 =$

- **F** 11,000
- **G** 10,105
- **H** 10,005
- **J** 10,033
- **K** None of these

GO

11

$8 - \frac{1}{8} =$

A $8\frac{1}{8}$
B $\frac{1}{7}$
C $7\frac{1}{8}$
D $7\frac{7}{8}$
E None of these

12

6 x 2.8 =

F 12.86
G 60
H 168
J 12.48
K None of these

13

11.9 + 6.4 =

A 17.3
B 18.3
C 5.5
D 17.94
E None of these

14

$4\overline{)76}$

F 19
G 18 R5
H 18 R6
J 18
K None of these

15

$$\begin{array}{r} \frac{2}{5} \\ + \frac{3}{10} \\ \hline \end{array}$$

A $\frac{7}{10}$
B $\frac{1}{3}$
C $\frac{7}{13}$
D $\frac{1}{10}$
E None of these

16

$\frac{3}{4} + \frac{5}{8} = \square$

F $\frac{1}{8}$
G $\frac{15}{32}$
H $1\frac{3}{8}$
J $\frac{8}{12}$
K None of these

17

$$\begin{array}{r} 6739 \\ + \ 7721 \\ \hline \end{array}$$

A 7257
B 1018
C 14,470
D 14,458
E None of these

18

10,000 − 5904 =

F 4096
G 5096
H 5904
J 15,904
K None of these

19

$$\begin{array}{r} 730 \\ \times \ 900 \\ \hline \end{array}$$

A 170
B 1630
C 657,000
D 973,000
E None of these

20

1072 ÷ 8 =

F 130 R4
G 134
H 133
J 13
K None of these

21 **For this problem, do <u>not</u> reduce your answer to lowest terms.**

$$\begin{array}{r} 7\frac{2}{14} \\ + \ \frac{5}{14} \\ \hline \end{array}$$

A $8\frac{2}{14}$
B $7\frac{8}{14}$
C 8
D $7\frac{7}{14}$
E None of these

STOP

Part 3 Applications

Examples

Directions: Find the correct answer to each problem. Mark the space for your choice.

E1

Railroad tracks are best described as real-world examples of —

A parallel lines

B perpendicular lines

C intersecting lines

D right angles

E2

A package weighs 4 pounds. The contents weigh 2.5 pounds. How much does the box weigh?

F 3.5 pounds

G 2.5 pounds

H 1.5 pounds

J 6.5 pounds

1 Which numbered triangle is similar to triangle A?

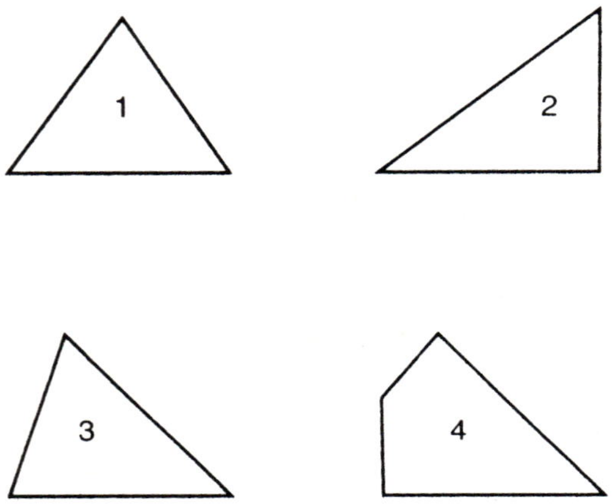

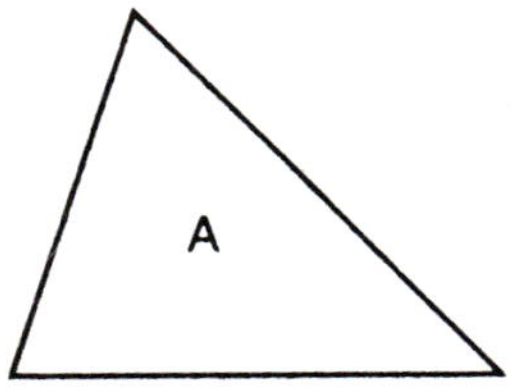

A 4

B 3

C 2

D 1

2 The perimeter of a square can be found by —

F dividing the length of a side by 4

G squaring the length of a side

H multiplying the length of a side by 4

J multiplying the length of a side by 6

3 What is the average length of a side of the figure below?

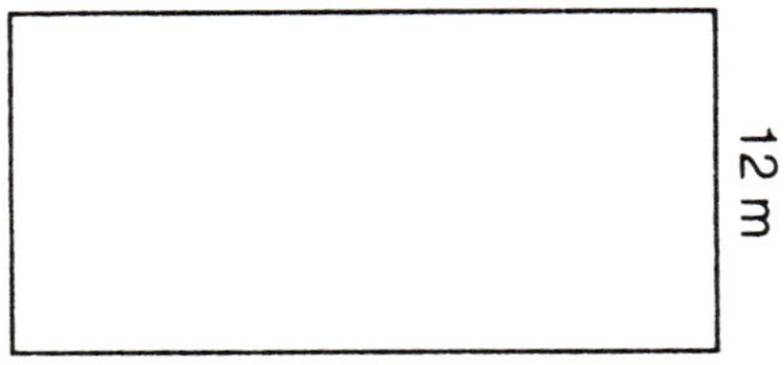

A 16 m

B 18 m

C 72 m

D 288 m

4 Half the students in a school are girls. One fourth of the girls play sports. If there are 720 students in the school, which of these would you use to find the number of girls who played sports?

F $720 \times \frac{1}{2} \times \frac{1}{4}$

G $720 \times \frac{1}{2} \times \frac{1}{2}$

H $720 \times \frac{4}{1} \times \frac{2}{1}$

J $720 \times \frac{1}{2} + \frac{1}{4}$

5 Which of these would best be used to measure the volume of a large bucket?

A yards

B grams

C liters

D pints

GO

The table below shows the price and monthly maintenance fees for several condominiums. Use the table to do numbers 6 through 8.

Condominium Costs and Fees			
Type	Square Feet	Cost	Monthly Fee
Efficiency	800	$85,000	$120
1 br, 1 bath	1200	$105,000	$135
2 br, 1 bath	1550	$135,000	$150
2 br, 2 baths	1550	$140,000	$180
3 br, 2 baths	1650	$165,000	$190
3 br, 3 baths	1750	$175,000	$200
4 br, 4 baths	2250	$200,000	$250
Free country club membership included on all units over $150,000.			

6 What is the least expensive type of condominium you could buy and still get a free country club membership?

F efficiency

G 1 br, 1 bath

H 3 br, 3 baths

J 3 br, 2 baths

7 What do you think the initials "br" mean in this table?

A bathroom

B bedroom

C weeks before renting

D browsing time

8 Suppose you and two friends bought a 3 br, 3 bath condomium and shared the monthly fees among yourselves. How much would each of you have to pay in fees for a whole year?

F $2400

G $1200

H $800

J $400

9 Carlos drives a truck for a delivery service. He averages 62 miles a day on weekdays and 45 miles on Saturday. About how far does he drive for work in 4 weeks?

A 1240 miles

B 355 miles

C 1420 miles

D 428 miles

10 Natasha is building her strength for the swimming season. She can now lift 75 pounds. She wants to increase the weight she can lift by 5 pounds a week for 6 weeks. At the end of 6 weeks, how much weight will she be able to lift?

F 105 pounds

G 30 pounds

H 92 pounds

J 80 pounds

11 A waterproof jacket costs $49.95. The cold-weather lining for the jacket is $22.50, and a matching hat is $12.75. How much would it cost to buy the jacket and liner, but not the hat?

A $85.20

B $72.45

C $61.45

D $62.70

12 What does the figure below show?

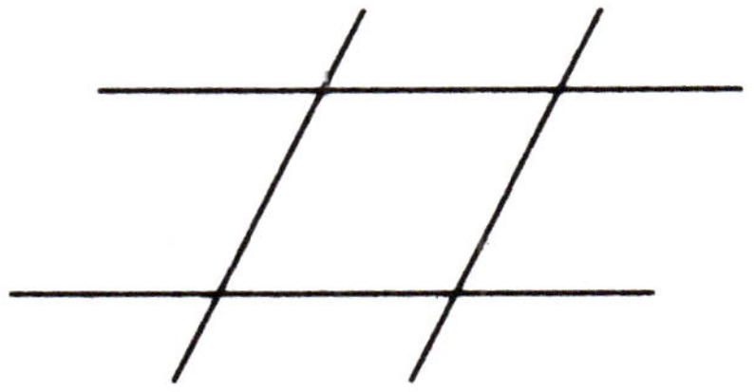

F four obtuse angles

G an acute square

H two pairs of right angles

J two pairs of parallel lines

13 A rectangular prism is 5 units wide, 8 units long, and 6 units high. What is it's volume?

A 88 cubic units

B 240 cubic units

C 256 cubic units

D 270 cubic units

14 This clock shows the time a bus reaches school. The first student gets on the bus at 7:35. How long does this student ride the bus before reaching school?

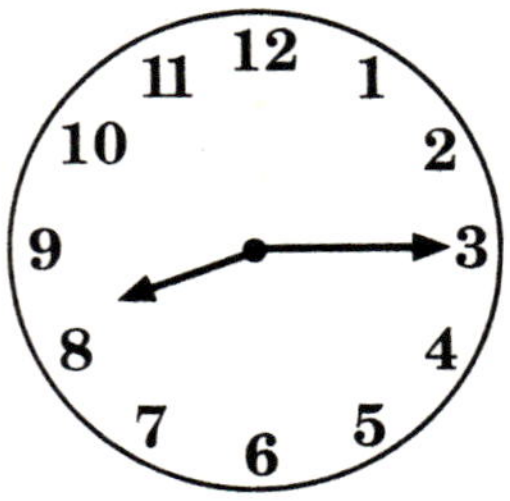

F 35 minutes

G 50 minutes

H 15 minutes

J 40 minutes

15 The Spanish Club wants to buy a set of instructional videos. Each video costs $12.50. What information will they need to determine how much money they must raise to buy the entire set of videos?

A The number of students in the school

B How long each video is

C The number of videos in the set

D How many students there are in the Spanish Club

16 Which of the shapes below can have only four faces?

F a pyramid

G a sphere

H a cube

J a rectangular prism

17 On a baseball diamond, it is 90 feet between each base, and there are four bases. Suppose a runner hits a double and has reached second base. How much farther does the runner have to go to reach home?

A 90 ft

B 180 ft

C 270 ft

D 360 ft

The graph below shows the total number of calories an athlete used while working out on Monday through Friday. Study the graph, then answer questions 18 and 19.

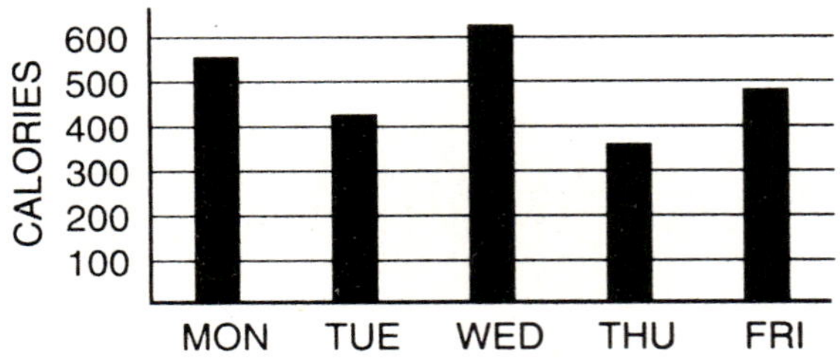

18 On which day did the athlete use about 475 calories during the workout?

F Wednesday

G Friday

H Tuesday

J Monday

19 This athlete knows that the food you eat 24 hours before a workout provides most of the energy for the workout. On what day should the athlete eat the most in order to have enough energy for the hardest workout?

A Wednesday

B Sunday

C Thursday

D Tuesday

GO

Use this graph to answer questions 20 through 23.

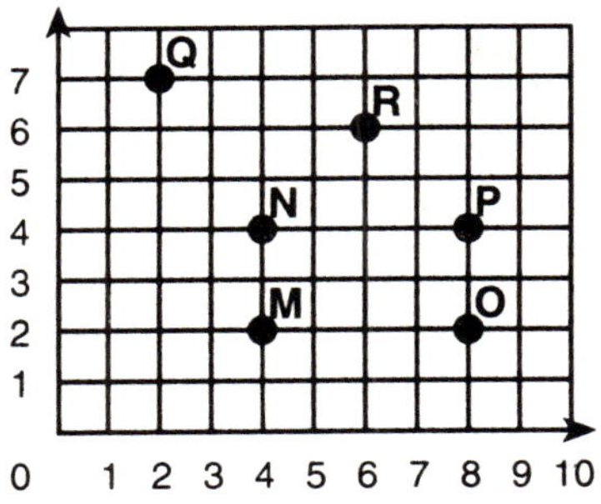

20 Which point is located at (4, 2)?

F P

G O

H N

J M

21 What are the coordinates of point P?

A (8, 4)

B (8, 2)

C (4, 8)

D (9, 5)

22 What shape is formed by joining points M, N, P, and O?

F triangle

G square

H rectangle

J trapezoid

23 Suppose you moved point Q down 2 units. What would the new coordinates be for point Q?

A (2, 9)

B (2, 5)

C (4, 7)

D (0, 2)

24 Which number sentence shows the perimeter of the square park below?

F 325 x 325 = ☐

G 2 x 325 = ☐

H 4 x 325 = ☐

J 4 + 325 = ☐

25 Which of these is the greatest distance?

A 5000 feet

B 2000 yards

C 1 mile

D 12,000 inches

26 Lake County has an area of 64 square miles. About 16 square miles of the county is made up of lakes. What is the ratio of water to land in the county?

F 4 to 1

G 1 to 4

H 3 to 1

J 1 to 3

27 In the figure below, the distance between each letter is the same. Which statement about the figure is true?

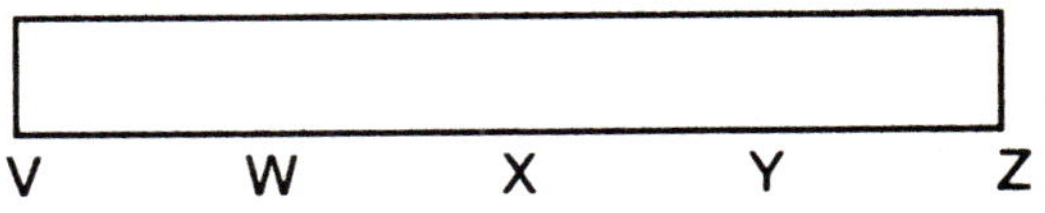

A Distance WY = 2 times Distance YZ

B Distance WY = Distance XY

C Distance VZ = 3 times Distance XY

D Distance YZ = Distance VX

STOP

Answer Keys

Reading
Unit 1,
Vocabulary
Lesson 1-pg.13
A B
B J
1 D
2 G
3 A
4 H
5 B
6 J
7 D
8 F
Lesson 2-pg.14
A B
B J
1 C
2 F
3 B
4 G
5 A
6 J
7 B
Lesson 3-pg.15
A A
B J
1 D
2 F
3 D
4 H
5 A
6 J
7 B
8 H
Lesson 4-pg.16
A D
B F
1 D
2 G
3 C
4 G
5 A
Lesson 5-pg.17
A D
B H
1 C
2 G
3 D
4 G
5 A
6 H
Lesson 6-pg.18
A D
B F
1 C
2 G
3 A
4 J
5 C
6 G
Lesson 7-pgs.19-22
E1 D
E2 G
1 A
2 H
3 D
4 F
5 B
6 G
7 C
8 G
9 C
10 F
11 B
12 J
13 C
14 J
15 C
16 G
17 A
18 J
19 B
20 G
21 D
22 G
23 C
24 H
25 B
26 H
27 D
28 G
29 A
30 H
31 A
32 J
33 C
34 F
35 B
Unit 2, Reading
Comprehension
Lesson 8-pg.23
A D
1 C
2 F
3 B
4 H
Lesson 9-pgs.24-27
A D
1 B
2 F
3 D
4 H
5 C
6 G
7 A
8 J
9 B
10 F
11 C
12 F
13 A
14 H
15 B
Lesson 10-pgs.28-33
A A
1 C
2 F
3 D
4 G
5 B
6 J
7 B
8 G
9 C
10 J
11 A
12 H
13 A
14 G
15 D
16 G
17 C
18 G
19 B
20 F
21 D
Lesson 11-pgs.34-42
E1 B
1 D
2 F
3 B
4 H
5 B
6 H
7 D
8 G
9 D
10 F
11 A
12 J
13 B
14 H
15 B
16 F
17 B
18 J
19 A
20 H
21 C
22 J
23 B
24 F
25 D
26 F
27 C
28 H
29 B
30 J
31 D
32 G
Unit 3, Test
Practice
Part 1-pgs.45-48
E1 B
E2 H
1 C
2 J
3 C
4 J

5	B
6	F
7	C
8	G
9	B
10	H
11	D
12	F
13	B
14	F
15	B
16	H
17	C
18	F
19	D
20	G
21	C
22	J
23	A
24	H
25	A
26	H
27	B
28	J
29	A
30	F
31	D
32	J
33	C
34	G
35	A

Test Practice
Part 2-pgs.49-57

E1	C
1	B
2	H
3	C
4	J
5	D
6	H
7	B
8	F
9	D
10	G
11	A
12	H
13	D
14	G
15	A
16	J
17	B
18	H
19	A
20	J
21	D
22	F
23	C
24	G
25	C
26	G
27	D
28	F

Language
Unit 1, Language Mechanics
Lesson 1-pgs.59-60

A	B
B	J
1	A
2	H
3	C
4	G
5	D
6	F
7	B
8	J
9	A
10	G
11	A
12	J
13	D
14	G
15	A
16	H

Lesson 2-pgs.61-63

A	A
B	J
1	C
2	G
3	D
4	J
5	A
6	H
7	C
8	J
9	B
10	F
11	D
12	G
13	A
14	H
15	B
16	F
17	D
18	H
19	C
20	F

Lesson 3-pgs.64-67

E1	D
1	A
2	H
3	D
4	G
5	A
6	H
7	B
8	J
9	B
10	H
11	C
12	F
13	D
14	G
15	A
16	H
17	D
18	F
19	D
20	H
21	B
22	H
23	A
24	J
25	B
26	F
27	C
28	J
29	B

Unit 2, Language Expression
Lesson 4-pgs.68-70

A	B
B	H
1	D
2	J
3	B
4	F
5	A
6	H
7	A
8	J
9	B
10	F
11	C
12	J
13	B
14	H
15	D
16	G
17	B
18	F
19	C
20	J

Lesson 5-pgs.71-73

A	A
B	G
C	D
1	A
2	F
3	C
4	G
5	C
6	G
7	D
8	F
9	C
10	G
11	C
12	J
13	C
14	F
15	B

Lesson 6-pgs.74-77

A	B
1	D
2	H
3	B
4	F
5	C
6	G
7	D
8	J
9	C
10	G
11	D
12	G
13	D
14	H

Lesson 7-pgs.78-81

E1	B
1	A
2	J
3	B
4	F
5	D
6	H
7	C
8	G
9	A
10	J
11	D
12	H
13	B
14	H

15 D
16 F
17 A
18 J
19 C
20 G

Unit 3, Spelling
Lesson 8-pgs.82-83

A A
B J
1 C
2 G
3 B
4 F
5 D
6 H
7 A
8 J
9 C
10 H
11 E
12 G
13 A
14 J
15 B
16 F
17 D
18 G

Lesson 9-pgs.84-85

E1 C
E2 G
1 D
2 G
3 B
4 F
5 C
6 G
7 A
8 J
9 C
10 J
11 E
12 F
13 C
14 J
15 B
16 F
17 A
18 J
19 B
20 H

Unit 4, Study Skills
Lesson 10-pgs.86-87

A D
1 C
2 F
3 B
4 J
5 B
6 H
7 A
8 G
9 D
10 G
11 D

Lesson 11-pgs.88-90

E1 D
E2 H
1 C
2 F
3 C
4 F
5 B
6 J
7 C
8 F
9 B
10 J
11 D
12 G
13 A
14 H
15 B
16 H

Unit 5, Test Practice
Part 1-pgs.93-95

E1 A
1 C
2 H
3 D
4 F
5 A
6 G
7 D
8 H
9 D
10 J
11 A
12 G
13 C
14 J
15 C
16 F
17 B
18 H
19 A
20 J
21 B

Test Practice
Part 2-pgs.96-99

E1 B
1 D
2 H
3 A
4 J
5 B
6 H
7 B
8 H
9 D
10 H
11 B
12 G
13 A
14 J
15 C
16 G
17 C
18 G
19 D
20 F

Test Practice
Part 3-pgs.100-101

E1 D
E2 F
1 D
2 F
3 C
4 H
5 B
6 F
7 D
8 G
9 A
10 H
11 D
12 G
13 E
14 G
15 A
16 J
17 A
18 J
19 B
20 F

Test Practice
Part 4-pgs.102-103

E1 A
1 D
2 G
3 C
4 F
5 D
6 H
7 C
8 F
9 D
10 H

Math
Unit 1, Concepts
Lesson 1-pgs.105-106

A C
B J
1 D
2 G
3 B
4 F
5 B
6 J
7 B
8 G
9 D
10 H
11 D
12 F
13 C
14 F

Lesson 2-pgs.107-108

A D
B F
1 B
2 F
3 C
4 J
5 C
6 G
7 D
8 H
9 A
10 H
11 A
12 J
13 B

Lesson 3-pgs.109-110

A B
B J
1 B
2 J
3 A
4 H
5 B
6 G

7 D
8 J
9 B
10 G
11 A
12 H
13 D

Lesson 4-pgs.111-112

A D
1 C
2 F
3 B
4 J
5 D
6 F
7 D
8 G
9 C
10 H
11 B
12 H

Lesson 5-pgs.113-114

E1 B
E2 F
1 D
2 G
3 A
4 F
5 C
6 H
7 A
8 H
9 D
10 G
11 B
12 H
13 A
14 G
15 D
16 H

Unit 2,
Computation

Lesson 6-pgs.115-116

A D
B K
1 C
2 F
3 D
4 J
5 E
6 J
7 C
8 F
9 C
10 K
11 C
12 G
13 A
14 J
15 A
16 J
17 D
18 G

Lesson 7-pgs.117-118

A D
B K
1 D
2 K
3 B
4 H
5 B
6 K
7 A
8 J
9 A
10 J
11 A
12 H
13 C
14 F
15 C
16 J
17 E
18 G

Lesson 8-pg.119

A E
B F
1 B
2 H
3 D
4 K
5 B
6 G
7 D
8 H

Lesson 9-pg.120

A C
B G
1 C
2 J
3 A
4 F
5 C
6 F
7 B
8 G

Lesson 10-pgs.121-122

E1 C
E2 K
1 B
2 K
3 D
4 F
5 C
6 J
7 E
8 F
9 B
10 H
11 A
12 J
13 A
14 H
15 C
16 K
17 B
18 H
19 E
20 F
21 B

Unit 3,
Applications

Lesson 11-pgs.123-126

A C
1 B
2 H
3 A
4 H
5 B
6 J
7 B
8 G
9 A
10 G
11 D
12 J
13 C
14 G
15 C
16 G
17 B
18 F
19 D
20 H
21 D
22 H

Lesson 12-pgs.127-130

A B
B J
1 B
2 J
3 B
4 F
5 D
6 F
7 C
8 G
9 B
10 H
11 D
12 G
13 D
14 H
15 D
16 F
17 C
18 F
19 C
20 J
21 B
22 J
23 C
24 F

Lesson 13-pgs.131-134

A A
B J
1 C
2 H
3 D
4 F
5 B
6 F
7 D
8 H
9 B
10 H
11 A
12 J
13 A
14 H
15 B
16 G
17 A
18 J
19 B
20 J
21 C
22 G
23 C

24 J
25 A

Lesson 14-pgs.135-138

E1	D
E2	G
1	D
2	F
3	C
4	G
5	A
6	H
7	C
8	F
9	B
10	F
11	D
12	G
13	B
14	J
15	D
16	G
17	C
18	J
19	B
20	H
21	B
22	G
23	C
24	H
25	D

Unit 4, Test Practice
Part 1-pgs.141-143

E1	C
E2	J
1	C
2	J
3	B
4	G
5	A
6	H
7	A
8	F
9	D
10	J
11	A
12	H
13	B
14	J
15	C
16	J
17	C
18	G
19	B
20	H
21	B
22	F
23	C
24	G
25	D

Test Practice
Part 2-pgs.144-145

E1	D
E2	K
1	B
2	J
3	E
4	J
5	A
6	J
7	A
8	G
9	B
10	G
11	D
12	K
13	B
14	F
15	A
16	H
17	E
18	F
19	C
20	G
21	D

Test Practice
Part 3-pgs.146-149

E1	A
E2	H
1	B
2	H
3	B
4	F
5	C
6	J
7	B
8	H
9	C
10	F
11	B
12	J
13	B
14	J
15	C
16	F
17	B
18	G
19	D
20	J
21	A
22	H
23	B
24	H
25	B
26	G
27	A

Reading Progress Chart

Circle your score for each lesson. Connect your scores to see how well you are doing.

Unit 1 Lesson 1	8 7 6 5 4 3 2 1
Lesson 2	7 6 5 4 3 2 1
Lesson 3	8 7 6 5 4 3 2 1
Lesson 4	5 4 3 2 1
Lesson 5	6 5 4 3 2 1
Lesson 6	6 5 4 3 2 1
Lesson 7	35 34 33 32 31 30 29 28 27 26 25 24 23 22 21 20 19 18 17 16 15 14 13 12 11 10 9 8 7 6 5 4 3 2 1
Unit 2 Lesson 8	4 3 2 1
Lesson 9	15 14 13 12 11 10 9 8 7 6 5 4 3 2 1
Lesson 10	21 20 19 18 17 16 15 14 13 12 11 10 9 8 7 6 5 4 3 2 1
Lesson 11	32 31 30 29 28 27 26 25 24 23 22 21 20 19 18 17 16 15 14 13 12 11 10 9 8 7 6 5 4 3 2 1

Language Progress Chart

Circle your score for each lesson. Connect your scores to see how well you are doing.

Unit 1 Lesson 1	Lesson 2	Lesson 3	Unit 2 Lesson 4	Lesson 5	Lesson 6	Lesson 7	Unit 3 Lesson 8	Lesson 9	Unit 4 Lesson 10	Lesson 11
16	20	29	20	15	14	20	18	20	11	16
15	19	28	19	14	13	19	17	19	10	15
14	18	27	18	13	12	18	16	18	9	14
13	17	26	17	12	11	17	15	17	8	13
12	16	25	16	11	10	16	14	16	7	12
11	15	24	15	10	9	15	13	15	6	11
10	14	23	14	9	8	14	12	14	5	10
9	13	22	13	8	7	13	11	13	4	9
8	12	21	12	7	6	12	10	12	3	8
7	11	20	11	6	5	11	9	11	2	7
6	10	19	10	5	4	10	8	10	1	6
5	9	18	9	4	3	9	7	9		5
4	8	17	8	3	2	8	6	8		4
3	7	16	7	2	1	7	5	7		3
2	6	15	6	1		6	4	6		2
1	5	14	5			5	3	5		1
	4	13	4			4	2	4		
	3	12	3			3	1	3		
	2	11	2			2		2		
	1	10	1			1		1		
		9								
		8								
		7								
		6								
		5								
		4								
		3								
		2								
		1								

Math Progress Chart

Circle your score for each lesson. Connect your scores to see how well you are doing.

Unit 1 Lesson 1	Lesson 2	Lesson 3	Lesson 4	Lesson 5	Unit 2 Lesson 6	Lesson 7	Lesson 8	Lesson 9	Lesson 10	Unit 3 Lesson 11	Lesson 12	Lesson 13	Lesson 14
14	13	13	12	16	18	18	8	8	21	22	24	25	25
13	12	12	11	15	17	17	7	7	20	21	23	24	24
12	11	11	10	14	16	16	6	6	19	20	22	23	23
11	10	10	9	13	15	15	5	5	18	19	21	22	22
10	9	9	8	12	14	14	4	4	17	18	20	21	21
9	8	8	7	11	13	13	3	3	16	17	19	20	20
8	7	7	6	10	12	12	2	2	15	16	18	19	19
7	6	6	5	9	11	11	1	1	14	15	17	18	18
6	5	5	4	8	10	10			13	14	16	17	17
5	4	4	3	7	9	9			12	13	15	16	16
4	3	3	2	6	8	8			11	12	14	15	15
3	2	2	1	5	7	7			10	11	13	14	14
2	1	1		4	6	6			9	10	12	13	13
1				3	5	5			8	9	11	12	12
				2	4	4			7	8	10	11	11
				1	3	3			6	7	9	10	10
					2	2			5	6	8	9	9
					1	1			4	5	7	8	8
									3	4	6	7	7
									2	3	5	6	6
									1	2	4	5	5
										1	3	4	4
											2	3	3
											1	2	2
												1	1